On the road to Rock & Roll there's a ... ,

Joe Strummer

Praise for *The Rise and Fall of the Clash*

'The whole story, warts 'n' all, told by those who knew them, those who were there and an on-form Jonesy recalling the eye of the most tumultuous hurricane ever to hit rock 'n' roll. An engrossing labour of love which does them proud.'

Kris Needs (author of *Joe Strummer and the Legend of the Clash* and *The Scream: the Music, Myths and Misbehaviour of Primal Scream*).

'*The Rise and Fall of the Clash* explores the evolution of the punk icons, from their early days … to their downward spiral'.

Rolling Stone Magazine

'*The Rise and Fall of the Clash* is a head-first plunge into conflict and chaos.'

The Boston Globe

'At times hilariously funny, *The Rise and Fall of the Clash* can also be heartrendingly sad…Garcia also scrupulously examines the role played in the Clash's last phase by the return of manager Bernard Rhodes'

Chris Salewicz (biographer of Joe Strummer, Mick Jagger and Keith Richards, Bob Marley, Jimmy Hendrix, Jim Morrison et al.)

'If you're looking for a definitive answer to the question "Whatever happened to The Clash?" then read this book!…It may, indeed, be "only rock'n'roll" but the human tragedy at the heart of this account is no less poignant because of it.'

Mike Laye, 'official' Clash photographer

The Rise and Fall

of

The Clash

By Danny Garcia

With an introduction by Tymon Dogg

THIN MAN PRESS

First Edition

Published in Great Britain in 2013 by Thin Man Press

Words Copyright © Danny Garcia 2012

Images by Mike Laye Copyright © Mike Laye 2012

Images by Joe Streno Copyright © Joe Streno 2012

A CIP catalogue record for this title is available from the British Library

ISBN 978-0-9562473-2-2

Thin Man Press, London

Part of Axis Agencies Ltd

axisagencies@btinternet.com

Contents

Foreword
by Chris Salewicz

Before Joe Strummer passed away in December 2002, the status of the Clash already had taken several quantum leaps; it had risen immeasurably since the days of the final line-up's miserable fading away in 1985. But it took Joe's shocking sudden death to make evident just how much he and the Clash were quietly, and very personally, revered in all quarters across this planet.

The final years of The Clash, however, from 1982 to 1985, took on weighty dimensions that could have fitted the plot-line of a Shakespearian tragi-comedy - with the weight falling mostly on the side of tragedy. This period forms the subject-matter of Danny Garcia's project, *The Rise and Fall of The Clash*.

The documentary expands on the content of Don Letts's *Westway to the World* – Letts, incidentally, has expressed admiration for Garcia's movie – and examines the cobweb-strewn labyrinths of the group's soul.

The Clash's firing of Mick Jones, the group's principal songwriter, ranks high in the annals of hubristic folly.

Joe Strummer and Paul Simonon knew it was essential to keep up the momentum of The Clash: so much had been achieved since the release of Combat Rock in April 1982. Yet it is apparent from the frequently exhausted, sometimes demented appearance of Joe Strummer that errors were made because everything was moving at such a pace that no-one had time to think. Danny Garcia's film reflects that era: at times hilariously funny, it can also be heartrendingly sad – as we see in the on-camera near-meltdown of guitarist Vince White, one of the two replacements for Mick Jones.

Garcia also scrupulously examines the role played in The Clash's last phase by the return of manager Bernie ('It's Bernard: I'm not a taxi-driver!') Rhodes. Rhodes once declared that The Clash should be like the Liverpool football team, in which the club was always greater than the individual members, and any member could be substituted.

The film concludes with a glance at Joe Strummer's subsequent career, with the Mescaleros. This formed part of the momentum of the return to favour of The Clash. Might Danny Garcia have a sequel planned? The Rise and Fall and Rise of The Clash?

Introducing the Cast
In order of appearance

Mick Jones

Michael Geoffrey "Mick" Jones (born 26 June 1955) was the guitar player/songwriter of The Clash until he was unceremoniously sacked in 1983 – an event that scandalized the Rock world. Jones went on to form Big Audio Dynamite with Don Letts before line-up changes led to the formation of Big Audio Dynamite II. Lately Jones played with Carbon Silicon along with Tony James and recently toured the world as part of the Gorillaz live band (which includes former Clash member Paul Simonon). Also reformed Big Audio Dynamite for a world tour and is currently gigging as Justice Tonight.

Terry Chimes

Terrence "Terry" Chimes (born 5 July 1956, Stepney, London) best known as the original drummer of The Clash. He later played with Johnny Thunders & The Heartbreakers, Hanoi Rocks, Billy Idol and Black Sabbath.

Tymon Dogg

Tymon Dogg (born Stephen John Murray in Formby, Lancashire, England) is a highly idiosyncratic English singer-songwriter and multi-instrumentalist, playing piano, violin, guitar, oud and a harp of his own invention. As well as developing his own solo sound, he worked with The Clash and later collaborated with Joe Strummer in The Mescaleros.

Pearl Harbor

Also known as Pearl E. Gates, Pearl was the lead singer of Pearl Harbor and the Explosions, a new wave band from San Francisco, California. Pearl was Clash bassist Paul Simonon's first wife.

Vince White

Gregory Stuart Lee White was born in Marylebone, London, in 1960. He is better known as Vince White, and was one of the guitar players recruited by The Clash to replace Mick Jones after he was fired from the band in 1983.

Nick Sheppard

Nick Sheppard is a Bristol-born guitarist. He was in the last line up of The Clash and also worked with The Cortinas, Head and, more recently, Australian band The DomNicks.

Pete Howard

Pete Howard is a Bath-born drummer who was recruited for The Clash's 1983 US Festival appearance in San Bernardino, California. The show was Mick Jones's last appearance with the band. Howard remained in the line-up until the end, in 1985. Howard has also worked with Eat.

Mickey Gallagher

Michael William Gallagher (born 29 October 1945 in Newcastle upon Tyne, England) is a British keyboard player, best known as a member of Ian Dury and the Blockheads. He also contributed to several Clash recordings.

Norman Watt-Roy

Norman Watt-Roy (born 15 February 1951, in Bombay – now Mumbai - India) is the bassist with The Blockheads. Watt-Roy also works with Wilko Johnson and contributed to recordings by The Clash.

Vic Godard

Vic Godard (born Victor John Napper in Southwest London, England) is a songwriter and lead singer of the punk group Subway Sect, another band managed by Bernie Rhodes.

Viv Albertine

Viv Albertine (born Viviane Katrina Louise Albertine in Australia 1955) is a British guitar player/singer-songwriter, best known as the guitarist in the all female punk group The Slits.

Ray Jordan

Raymond Jordan was the man in charge of security in The Clash camp. He also worked for The Police, The Pretenders and Big Audio Dynamite amongst other bands.

Jock Scot

Poet and friend of the band, Jock was an insider in The Clash's inner circle from the late seventies until the very end.

Dan Donovan

Daniel Donovan (born 9 August 1967) is a British photographer and keyboard player, probably best known for being a member of Big Audio Dynamite. Following a brief stint in 1990 with The Sisters of Mercy he became a founding member of Dreadzone.

Chris Salewicz

Author and journalist, Chris Salewicz has documented popular culture for over three decades, in print and on television and radio. Author of *Redemption Song: The Ballad of Joe Strummer.*

Kris Needs

Kris Needs (born 2 July 1954) is a British journalist and author, primarily known for his writings on the music scene from the 1970s onwards. Author of *Joe Strummer and the Legend of The Clash.*

Fayney

Michael Fayne started his musical career working with The Clash in Camden Town's Rehearsal Rehearsals as a sound engineer. He later worked with projects like Roachford.

Barry 'Scratchy' Myers

Barry Myers AKA Scratchy was the DJ chosen by Joe Strummer to tour with The Clash in the United States and beyond back in 1979. Scratchy continues with his DJ-ing career today.

Rudy Fernandez

Rudy 'Can't Fail' Fernandez was the man in San Francisco for The Clash. Purveyor of herbs and other forms of entertainment in the Bay Area, Rudy remains a personal friend of the band since 1979.

Mark Helfond

Bernie Rhodes' right hand man and also the man in charge of the Clash office in New York 1982/1983.

Jesús Arias

Rock journalist and personal friend of Joe Strummer. From Granada, Spain.

Mike Laye

Mike was the last in-house photographer of The Clash and worked with Bernie Rhodes managing Subway Sect in 1978.

Chris Townsend

The man behind 5th Column, the manufacturers of most Clash merchandise in the late seventies and early eighties.

Introduction

By Tymon Dogg

This book could just as well have been called the Fall then the Rise of the Clash given the ever increasing significance of their music and the place the band now occupies in Rock and Roll history.

The Clash, as a band, have rarely been as revered and sincerely loved as they are now, thirty years on.

Whatever personal differences they had just confirm that these were real people who had real character issues and that they were not willing to hide them for mercenary reasons.

It is a fact of life that plastic flowers outlive real ones...

For myself, I knew Joe Strummer from 1971; we lived in the same house and played music together; when he met Mick and the Clash started rehearsing I was struck by the open-mindedness and lack of self-importance in the band. We sometimes had fierce arguments though, about what was empty fashion and what was real innovation.

I saw them play live on several occasions, first with Pablo LaBritain (later of 999) on drums, then Terry Chimes. While some of the material was raw back then, I could hear they knew how to swing a fourth from the tune of *White Riot.*

From 1978 to 1980 I didn't see much of them because I was living in the North but I remember when *London Calling* came out I heard it in a Newcastle record store. The B-side, *Armagideon Time,* really struck me with that opening line - 'A lot of people won't get no supper tonight' – and I knew, as did their fans, that they had not left their creative roots.

From their first album, *The Clash,* they included songs that were written by other artists. Songs that spoke of politics or emotions they empathized with; they wanted to share the position and influence they had built and let people hear what these other artists were giving. In the same way that the Rolling Stones used to get exposure for Blues artists.

In 1980, when they had cracked the US charts and had all of America talking about them, I worked with Joe, Topper, Mick and

Paul. I was involved in *Sandinista* and *Combat Rock*... they were working at breakneck speed to get as much musical inspiration recorded as they could and they opened the doors to many other musicians to help make the collective better. This took both wisdom and humility.

They were open to many kinds of inspiration, from Jazz to Reggae. *Look Here* by Mose Allison was on *Sandinista* for example, and Mikey Dread worked closely with Paul, bringing the resonance and weight of reggae to the band.

Repetition was not an option for the Clash. *Somebody Got Murdered* and *Charlie Don't Surf* have wonderful, almost psychedelic, guitar pop tunes. Joe's line from the latter, 'everybody wants to rule the world', got nicked by Tears for Fears. Joe met them sometime later and said 'you must owe me at least a fiver for that line...give us a fiver for that line' and they did.

For any group of people to do anything together that works depends on them being true, inspired individuals to start with – and that's a kind of contradiction because any artist is privileged with (and defined by) his or her own point of view.

Paul, Mick and Joe worked together from 1976 to 1983 (with Topper joining in 1977). This is actually not that much shorter a time than the Beatles worked together.

Each member of the band brought to the collective particular, essential ingredients:

Topper brought a wide knowledge and understanding of rhythm; and he was really precise when it came to producing the rhythmic core that is essential to rock music.

Paul had great artistic flair and an instinctive awareness of what music would get to the generation that he was very much part of, being only nineteen when he joined the band.

Mick had a genuine knowledge and love of song writing, and particularly songs that captured the pop cultural mood. Mick wrote songs that were deceptively simple but all musicians know that to write a simple tune that catches peoples' attention is one of the hardest things in the world.

Joe had lived in a ruggedness that only authentic songs could survive.

To have one strong song writer and singer in a band is essential but to have two who can work together is a rare formula…that's downright fortunate for all involved, it's a turbo-band.

This was the collective power of the Clash.

When the Clash achieved the position of mega-stars it went against their natural instincts as individuals in what appears to be a spiritual democracy. They didn't feel comfortable in the role of leading other people. They set about their work as artists expressing themselves and didn't expect this to confer on them some kind of superior significance as human beings.

The Rock'n'Roll game did not see them betray their creative instincts.

The body of work – five albums – voiced the progress of a generation. Although there was only eleven years between John Lennon and Joe Strummer, each was a sincere commentator on, and critic of, what was going on for their peers.

Financial success and material excesses were not considered trophies of artistic prowess by our generation. It was much more important to feel a creative dialogue and respect between yourself (as an artist) and each individual in the audience. Clash fans felt very much that the music was an honest conversation with human beings they may or may not meet.

At the beginning of the 1980s machines entered music.

Synthesizers couldn't mimic God-given instruments such as violin or acoustic guitar, but they accurately reproduced the sound of pianos and trumpets. The most significant development was the drum machine which could be programmed by someone who couldn't even keep the most rudimentary beat. Now all musicians and producers, who had previously relied on human feeling to produce the beats that expressed an emotion, had to hand a machine that could keep so-called 'perfect timing' forever.

Mick saw a future in this for rap music and dance music. Joe had an aversion to all things mechanical. This was a significant creative difference.

Many artists who refused to contemplate using drum machines went through some hard years, like Joni Mitchell and Leonard Cohen - who was dropped by his record company – and quite a lot of rock bands. Real drummers sweat real time yet many of them worried they'd be out of work

Topper's well-documented exit from the band left them without the means to combat this onslaught of computer back-beat.

As the Clash were intrinsically human, to make this jump into machines was impossible for all of them...except Mick.

Mick proved his vision with Big Audio Dynamite.

Joe proved his vision with the 1987 soundtrack he did for the film *Walker* and his work with *The Mescaleros*, where he felt comfortable, was genuinely happy and buoyant and which he later said was the best work he had ever done. It was as a member of *The Mescaleros* that I was fortunate enough to renew my friendship and shared vision with Joe.

The survival of things doesn't mean they are profound. An ashtray will outlive the smoker.

Longevity is not justification for boring repetition and amassing unnecessary material goods; awareness of these simple facts was very much what triggered the emergence of punk – or, indeed, any kind of new music.

Many have attempted to analyze The Clash's enduring appeal four decades on. The music seems to be gathering more mystique and significance; there probably isn't a contemporary song at the moment that can better sum up the feeling of the 2011 riots than *Know Your Rights* with Joe's hoarse voice screaming 'get off the streets'.

For all the Clash's image-making they were very much - along with the Sex Pistols – anti-Rock Stars.

Joe always remained accessible and did 'endless interviews', but he couldn't see the point of de-humanizing himself to become more famous and more rich. In fact none of the Clash members wanted the excessive Rock lifestyle epitomized by the previous generation of 'rock stars' so far as I could see.

The management was in tune with this feeling, from straight-talking Bernie Rhodes to the very humane Peter Jenner.

The Clash were extremely judgmental of each other if anyone slipped from an almost saintly reaction to their celebrity and the mass hysteria they inspired. People became infatuated with them, it's true - within a week of Joe's death 80,000 messages of condolence had been sent – but at the heart of this affection was recognition of, and trust in, the band's integrity.

Other artists were also won over by their unpretentiousness; musicians, writers, film directors and film stars became friends and admirers. Years ago in New York, the great poet Alan Ginsberg joined them onstage at Bond's and the whole band spontaneously backed him for ten minutes. More recently, I noticed that in the 2011 film *Moneyball* Brad Pitt has a poster of the Clash in the background; Pitt also encouraged the use of the Mescaleros' song *Mondo Bongo* in the film that saw him and Angelina Jolie fall in love, *Mr and Mrs Smith*.

Joe's reaction watching someone getting into a big limo to take them home was 'and what are they trying to prove?' At the height of the Clash's success, Joe's girlfriend Gabby used to pick him up in a Morris Minor. At the time I used to drive around in a Reliant Regal three-wheeler and Mick told me he had more respect for it than for any flash ego-boosting car. He and his then girlfriend, Ellen Foley, used to get a lift with me even though it usually meant they'd end up having to push the car to get it started. They didn't feel they needed materialism to express their success. In fact they felt very uncomfortable about that aspect of their lives and their argument was more about who felt the most uncomfortable.

I remember Joe arriving at a party after he'd been to a Rolling Stones gig. He said 'they were playing a stadium! That's it, they're finished, the Rolling Stones are so crap.' We argued, I was saying 'What so *Exile on Main Street* is crap, you saw them in a stadium and now *Street Fighting Man* is crap?' But that was how he felt at that time – of course he later played stadium gigs himself, both with The Clash and the Mescaleros.

Looking back, it appears that the Clash were on the brink of U2-size superstardom and some might think they were foolish to let the band fall apart; but in fact, as human beings, it was possibly the wisest thing they ever did. What seems foolish to a lot of strangers is not foolish to the people living the reality. Living your life according to the evaluation of others can be very destructive to the soul.

The fact that the work lives on is a testament to the vision, honesty and integrity of The Clash and everyone who helped them along the way.

Everybody looks for something of themselves in other people, and a lot of people still see themselves in The Clash.

As I see it, it will be the Rise and Rise of The Clash until someone comes up with a better way to Rock and Roll.

Tymon Dogg, London, November 2012

How My Film Got Made

By Danny Garcia

On the road to Rock & Roll there's a lot of wreckage in the ravine...

Joe Strummer

1. I'm not Down

Picture a nine year old boy on his bicycle singing "Spanish Bombs" in a hot Spanish summer afternoon. It's 1980 and the boy is me.

Eleven years later I tell Paul Simonon the anecdote and he's taken aback, I can tell by the look on his face that he sees this as a real compliment, one he didn't expect.

Eighteen years after that, I'm talking to Mick Jones telling him the same story and he just grins, toking a spliff under the Welsh Moon. I literally grew up with the music of The Clash thanks to my brother Sergi and his cassette collection.

When I started this Clash documentary project it was purely an act of desperation. I was coming out of a depression that had lasted too long when I came across Vince White's book *Out Of Control, the last days of The Clash* on the internet.

Previously I had done four documentaries for BTV, a local TV station that used to lend video cameras to people with ideas (not necessarily journalists or professional cameramen, and I was neither) and let them run free in the streets of Barcelona.

The first thing I did was email Vince and to my surprise he responded in the affirmative very quickly. The next person I got in touch with was the legendary two time manager of the band, Bernie Rhodes.

Bernie, or Bernard as he prefers to be called these days, also managed The Specials, Dexy's Midnight Runners and The Subway Sect amongst others. At first he was puzzled by my idea and proposed that if I came to London he would meet me for a coffee and discuss the project further face to face. That meeting never took place.

After I got in touch with Bernie I started to chase the great Mickey Gallagher, the keyboard player for the Blockheads and fifth Clash member in 1980-81, personally my favorite Clash period. Mickey gave the band an extra ingredient that added much depth and melody to their music as well as bringing **'the funk into them'** as he puts it.

During the first weeks of research I managed to get contact details for Mike Laye, the last in-house photographer of The Clash and ex Subway Sect minder. Not only that, he knew Bernie from the early days of Punk as he worked in the ICA Theatre and was responsible for putting together one of the first shows The Clash ever did. He became friends with Joe and Paul, and stayed that way until the end of the band.

Another interesting fellow I got in touch with early on was Michael Fayne aka Fayney, the man behind the dreadful drum machine patterns recorded all over *Cut the Crap*, the last album of The Clash, **'I didn't have any talent then... I do now!'** Fayney excused himself.

I bought that album back in '86 and I grew up completely intrigued by that last line up. Who were these new guys? The look of that guy playing cards on the right (Vince White) was very contrived, he didn't even look right for The Clash. His style was more like that of a Camden Town Punk stall mannequin instead of the classic Clash cool look we were used to. Mohawk, bullet belt... naff. Unfortunately, pretty much in tune with the contents of the record.

In 1991 I interviewed Paul Simonon when he came to Barcelona with Havana 3AM and I told him I was still trying to figure out what had happened with the end of The Clash. During the interview he kept his cool but backstage after the show he looked very depressed when we spoke about the end of the band and not only that, he was very disappointed about the whole thing. I tried to cheer him up reminding him about the double and triple albums at discount prices and the benefit shows and so on and he replied about growing up with heroes such as Lawrence of Arabia and that perhaps his aims were too high and that the Clash **'could**

have done something great for the people but perhaps we were just a Rock & Roll band'.

When I asked him if he knew the new guys in the band (Vince, Nick and Pete) he said **'No!'** and then I asked him: **'so was it all a set-up?'** and he replied: **'That's it!'**

2. First Night Back in London

Bernie Rhodes knows, don't argue

Gangsters, The Specials

I was beginning to enjoy my detective work, tracing all these middle aged men that at some point had been involved with the last great Rock & Roll band on Earth, so with a handful of contacts and 500€ in my pocket (courtesy of my backers) I flew to London and continued with my research.

Right after landing in Stansted I took the train to Liverpool Street and went straight into Foyles in Charing Cross Road and other book shops around it to acquire books such as Johnny Green's *A Riot Of our Own, Night And Day With The Clash* or Chris Salewicz's *Redemption Song* before heading to Camden Town to enjoy a hot cappuccino in my favorite Spanish joint in London - Bar la Gansa in Inverness Street, just down the road from Rehearsal Rehearsals.

It was January 16th 2009 and London was freezing. As the Evening Standard described it next day: 'Minus 10 degrees, Artic temperatures in Trafalgar Square!'. Not fun.

I had ten days to meet and convince a bunch of people to help me with this project.

The problem was that I was a nobody in the film industry (still am) but these guys didn't seem to mind my skimpy resumé, except for Bernie that is.

In my first hour-long conversation on the phone with Bernie I had to explain myself to him in a way I had never done with anyone before, not even with police or custom officers. Questions like **'what was your father? What did your father do?'** were coming out of the telephone line.

Obviously Bernie was still puzzled not so much by my project but by me. Who was this guy coming out of nowhere with this crazy idea almost 25 years after the demise of the last Clash line up? And most important: what social class did I belong to? That seems to be very important for Bernie and he couldn't figure out my upbringing through my accent. According to Bernie if you are working class you are cool but if you are middle class you better come up with something outstanding or you'll be categorized as a 'rich cunt' which is what happened to Vince, Pete and Nick.

My father's revolutionary past didn't impress Bernie and he made an excuse not to meet me but agreed to call me back in a week while I was still in London.

The second conversation with Bernie was much more interesting. The first thing he said was: **'I didn't fire Mick! It was Joe and his hippie friends that did it! Because you know Joe had all these hippie friends around'.** You could feel right from the start his manipulative ways were at work. The chat lasted for an hour in which Bernie praised himself for having created The Clash, and putting Run DMC and Aerosmith together **('that singer wants $500 right? We'll give him 1000 and he'll be just happy to do it you know?')**, giving Public Enemy their look and vision **('who do you think did that huh?')** and telling me of his love for Spain and how the Guardia Civil arrested him in the 60's for vagrancy and kept him inside for a few days for being a long-haired hippie.

When I confronted him with reports that he paid Vince and the new guys measly wages he blamed Strummer again saying **'it was Joe who wanted to put them through the loop, he didn't want to give it all to them that easy',** mixed with the classic manager rap of **'I was putting money in their pockets every week, buying them the clothes they wanted...what would you say to that?'** waiting for me to just agree with him. I realized I was becoming *Bernified* fast, I had to snap out of it but this little fellow was too good to listen to. In between all the self-praising stuff there might be some truth, who knows?

Then he went on to analyze Vince, Pete and Nick one by one and what they had achieved after their brief spell in The Clash and for some reason he was still bashing Vince comparing his poor musical career with the other two: 'at least **Pete played with that band... Eat**' and finally pointing out that the three of them together '**should have done their own band**' after Joe quit The Clash.

It was clear Bernie didn't like my project and at first I didn't understand why, after all I was going to talk about the album he had helped create and if I used some music from it in the film I was going to make him a bit of money through publishing royalties. Nobody can forget the fact that, when Joe split after recording most of his part, Bernie finished *Cut the Crap* with Fayney, Nick Sheppard and Vince. Under the pseudonym José Unidos, Bernie produced the album and CBS put it out with all the songs being (unconvincingly) credited to: Strummer/ Rhodes.

The question that has to be asked is: who was responsible for quality control at CBS UK in 1985?

Rock history is littered with cases in which managers have taken it too far and steered their clients' careers down roads they would never have gone by themselves. Bernie's story seemed to me like a classic example of this, but a part of me wanted to listen to the guy's explanations and perhaps learn something new. At the end of the day I was just beginning to figure out what really had gone down. Plus, if I wanted to do an exhaustive and thorough investigation I had to leave my opinions out of it and listen to every single suspect with an open mind, giving them the benefit of the doubt.

Bernie was curious when I told him I played the bass. When he asked me '**why the bass?**' I forgot to tell him I grew up with images of Sid Vicious, Dee Dee Ramone and Paul Simonon swinging their white Fender P's with the black scratcher... the coolest bass guitar ever made... instead I just told him '**it felt good**', which was also the truth, as it is the fact that is easier to play than the guitar, any child can do it.

I always dreamed I'd play in The Clash when I was a kid. I also dreamed of playing for FC Barcelona one day and that didn't happen either.

But while it didn't happen to me and thousands of other dreamers, it did somehow happen for Vince White and those two other two fellows, Pete Howard and Nick Sheppard.

Pete still lives in London and became the drummer in Queenadreena whereas Nick settled in Australia with his family and plays guitar in local bands.

So the day came when I would meet Vince White, the mohicaned guitar player that looked out of place in The Clash, even in the dodgy Clash he looked dodgy! How could that be possible?   Well it was totally possible and you just need to look at a few pictures to realize he didn't belong next to Joe and Paul. The boots he wore were wrong, his haircut was wrong from day one, his choice of guitar, his fucking bullet belt, everything about him screamed 'phony!'. I can't believe neither Joe, Paul nor Kosmo spotted those facts! I mean Paul was supposed to be the tasty artsy guy, he must have noticed something was wrong with him from day one besides his real name being Gregory. Maybe they did notice but they were desperate for another guitar replacement?

The smell of hot dogs and cheap fast food was running down Ladbroke Grove like a bad virus while I smoked a joint waiting for Vince. Fifteen minutes late his sad figure emerged through the West London artery and soon we were walking down the Grove and into The Elgin, one of the local pubs where Joe had played with The 101'ers back in the day.

Vince looked damaged in his old beaten up black leather jacket; after reading his book I understood how mind boggling that experience must have been for him. According to his book, Vince was bullied from the start and took the blame for a lot of shit; his guitar was so low on the mix when playing live that he could barely hear his solos, his guitar playing was constantly criticized and overall it all seemed like it was a devastating experience during which his self-esteem was battered and bruised for two whole years.

It seemed like The Clash was 'his Vietnam' because he sure looked like a war veteran. The biggest flakes of dandruff I have ever seen were hanging from his hair, the skin around his nose was all dry and he stank of alcohol.

Vince is a very bitter man. On one hand he still loves Joe and must feel proud to have once been associated with the legendary front man, on the other hand there's rage inside that man. A profoundly rooted hatred for Bernie and also for Joe, for allowing

Bernie to get away with *Cut the Crap* and ultimately destroying the band.

When I ask him about The Elgin being a classic Clash boozer he says **'with Joe, every boozer was a Clash boozer'** and claims that **'Joe wanted me in the band because I was an alcoholic because you know he was an alcoholic, right?'**.

I have heard different versions of the story and different people have told me different things but one thing is for sure, when I met Joe in 1999 and spend a few hours hanging out with him and The Mescaleros crew he wasn't drinking at all.

When I fronted Vince with the question of why he stayed in such miserable circumstances, under such pressure and earning such shitty wages while Joe, Paul and Bernie were getting good money he just said: **'but you don't understand! I was in The Clash!'**. I wanted to say he 'wasn't really in The Clash' but I didn't. The way he said it was as if he had played with The Rolling Stones for a couple of years. I was beginning to grasp the drama of Vince's aftermath. He is another casualty in the list of victims that suffered from The Clash 'Juju'.

I spent a couple of hours talking to Vince, telling him about my project and paying for his pints of lager. It was pretty much clear that he had said it all in his book and there wasn't much extra information I could get from him, not even Pete's contact details which he had misplaced or lost, perhaps he never had them in the first place.

Luckily for me, one of my contacts passed me Pete's phone number and I tried to set up an interview with him while I was in London. After a failed attempt, I finally got hold of him in the pub-restaurant he manages these days and spoke to him for a good forty minutes about the project and his role in the band as the bridge between the two incarnations of the Clash. We spoke about Vince, his relationship with him and Nick Sheppard, Topper's drumming abilities and...the US Festival. When I asked him if he knew Bernie charged half a million dollars for that show while he got paid just $300 he just laid his head between his arms, shaking it from side to side, going: **'don't tell me about it'**.

Pete didn't have kind words for Bernie either, but he certainly wasn't as disturbed by the whole experience as Vince; Pete seemed to have been OK after the Clash ordeal, perhaps a little pissed off by the way things went down but that was almost 25 years ago and sometimes it's best to let things go.

Pete mentioned that a guy called Eddie had often filmed them at sound-checks, on the tour bus, etc. and that I should contact him; Eddie also used to do all the in house artwork for Bernie around that period.

Before I left London again, I had time to meet someone else who was involved with The Clash, not only for the band's last two years of existence but since the late seventies. He is responsible for the *Sandinista*, *Combat Rock* and *Cut the Crap* covers amongst many other things that he has done in the Clash catalogue over the years, his name: Jules Balme.

After about a dozen phone calls he agreed to meet me in The Prince Albert, a pub in Notting Hill.

Balme had never been involved in any Clash documentary or book and I was pretty sure he had a few stories to tell. Over a Bloody Mary, Balme told me how Bernie and Kosmo had wanted to recreate the old band camaraderie with the new guys but obviously the vibe wasn't there. **'I can see they were trying to get that band feel back with that trip to Bristol, but it wasn't working,'** he said referring to a sudden trip to the West Country that Bernie put together almost like a school outing. On board were a couple of journos from the Los Angeles Times who in their article quoted Kosmo saying **'See, even socialists can have fun!'** while having a good old time at one of Bristol's hippest joints.

Balme confirmed that the guy I wanted to talk to was Eddie…and that his surname was King. Balme explained that by 1984 he was too busy to do everything Bernie wanted from him so Eddie did stuff too while Jules concentrated on the big things - album covers mainly.

Balme also explained to me how Bernie flew him to New York days before the Shea Stadium show because the manager was negotiating a compilation album with CBS (or Epic in the US) and he would be required to come up with the artwork there and then.

The compilation never happened but Balme remembered Bernie trying to make him chose whether **'The Clash or Adam & The Ants'** were more important to him, referring to Jules' then recent work for the latter.

Balme also told me about the huge amounts of cash they were making from merchandise in that period. **'And most important'** he said, **'They kept the brand alive for an extra two years'**, referring to the days of The Clash II and probably meaning: they made much more than you think.

He made a mention of seeing The Clash mark II live in Brixton saying **'it was alright you know? I mean Mick wasn't there... there was one of the new guys singing *Police On My Back* which was a bit strange...it wasn't the same but it was alright I suppose!'**. He didn't look too convinced by his own words as he swallowed the last drops of his Bloody Mary before heading off to a meeting while promising to contact Kosmo on my behalf and explain the project to him.

I was getting closer to the top of the pyramid but there was still a long way to go.

3. Killing Time

Back in Spain the research continued, I spoke to Sony, various newspapers, photographers, TV stations, footage owners, fans, writers and finally I got through to the band's current manager, Tricia Ronane.

Ronane's advice was curt and to the point. She told me I should just stop the project at once since the band would not be granting me **'any rights for any Clash music';** but since this is a detective movie more than a glorification of the band's musical legacy, I responded that I didn't need any music to tell the story and that I'd have my lawyers talk to theirs and we'd let them have a big lawyer talk.

Away from their 'control' I was free to do the unauthorized documentary I was looking to make, not the bubblegum stuff the public was getting used to.

Plus I had a Plan B and a Plan C for the soundtrack so I started to contact artists such as Willi Williams, the writer of *Armagideon Time*, Danny Ray, the man who wrote and sang *Revolution Rock* and also Sonny Curtis himself, the legendary composer of *I Fought The*

Law and Buddy Holly's right hand. The buzz those emails gave me kept on fueling my ambitions through a period that would be prove to be one of the most difficult in the making of this film.

Somebody that made me understand I should stick with the unauthorized version was David Mingay, the co-creator of *Rude Boy*, the documentary he filmed in 78 and 79 with his partner Jack Hazan, which has since become a classic in The Clash universe.

Mingay was adamant that I should only do an unauthorized version so I could tell the truth for once: **'that's the film I'd go to see!'** he said on the phone sounding very enthusiastic. He offered his help for anything I would need in the future.

Another breakthrough came soon afterwards when one Sunday morning I was awakened by the sound of my cellphone. I looked at the caller ID and saw that it was a UK number; when I answered I recognized the voice of none other than legendary road manager turned writer: Mr. Johnny Green.

Johnny's call was another boost of energy to my plans and I could feel the project was gaining momentum every day. Johnny sounded very interested in the project and he also had unanswered questions like **'what was Paul doing auditioning singers?'**, referring to the last attempt at saving the band in late 85 or early 86 when they were looking for a replacement for Joe Strummer.

Sad, sad, sad.

No wonder Paul felt disappointed with the whole thing.

For the next two months I pestered Johnny on the blower trying to get me an OK or a fuck you from Mick, Topper and Paul. It was impossible. Although he still acts as the liaison between the world and the band members, it was very hard for me to get him to agree that he would talk to the guys on my behalf. Instead he told me to show up in Wales where he was going to interview Mick and Topper live onstage at the Laugharne Festival. There I could pitch my documentary and talk to them face to face.

During the two months I had to wait until that date in April, I finally got in touch with Eddie King. He told me that the footage he filmed in the US tour of 84 was made to be shown on the TV screens they had on stage that year and that Bernie kept everything when he decided to leave The Clash camp. Eddie's best-known work for The Clash is the cover of the *Know Your Rights* single and the *Straight To Hell* 12-inch, featuring a skull wearing a war helmet next to four aces.

Recently, Eddie has been involved in a lawsuit that involves his work in the past. Mainly because of this, Eddie refused to be interviewed for my project.

The first time I spoke to Mike Laye he said a couple of things that really stuck in my mind and that would steer me onto the right path. While talking about Bernie he said: **'I don't know whether Bernie did things out of greed or incompetence'** and remembering one of those photo sessions with the band he said **'with the new guys and his orange mohawk Joe was looking like an older guy trying to look young and that was sad'**. He also remembers telling Joe: **'you have a baby now, why don't you take it easy and forget about this Rock & Roll stuff?'** But Joe was having none of it; **'he was very excited saying it was great now to play with the new guys because they brought this fresh energy'**.

I now had around 20 potential interviewees and things were looking up when I finally got through to Nick Sheppard, the Bristol-based ex-Cortinas guitarist. He too seemed interested in the film and we started to email each other, trying to figure out the best way to meet up for an interview.

Around the same period I got in touch with people like Don Letts, Caroline Coon, Ellen Foley, Vic Goddard, Kris Needs, Jock Scot, Terry Chimes, Chris Salewicz, Barry "Scratchy" Myers and Robin Banks, all of whom showed an interest in the project.

The list of interviewees kept growing but still no sign of Jones, Topper or Simonon...these guys were as hard to reach as the goddamn Rolling Stones!

The Clash truly penetrated the very fabric of society with *Combat Rock* and were now iconic specially since Joe's passing in 2002. Now Joe was Saint Strummer...but where were all these fans when Earthquake Weather came out in 89? I was one of the 7,000 people on Earth that bought that album back then, in fact I bought two copies, vinyl and CD.

That just shows how important and how big The Clash were as a vehicle for Joe's ideas and that the sum of the four of them would always be infinitely superior to anything they would do separately. Only Mick Jones achieved certain success with Big Audio Dynamite through the 80's and 90's while Joe struggled with soundtracks and small roles in independent movies, Topper fought his heroin habit and Paul focused mainly on his artwork when the Havana 3AM project folded after Nigel Dixon's premature death.

One thing I want to say about Topper is that in 1986, during a brief respite from his self-imposed exile from the music scene, he produced what it is to me the best album ever made by an ex-Clash member, the almost forgotten *Waking Up*. A delicious collection of soul numbers that was perhaps too good for its time.

4. This is England

April was now around the corner and I managed to secure the money I needed to get over to Wales and show up at that festival Johnny Green had told me about.

I decided to drive my little proletariat car up to Wales so I could stop on my way in the small French town where Mike Laye lives these days and then film a bit of Paris before heading up to Wales and London where I would be conducting most of the interviews for the documentary.

Mike turned out to be one of the nicest people I have encountered while doing this project and his interview was even better than I expected. He encouraged me to go on with my quest for the truth, and told me about his friendship with Joe. Mike lived in Notting Hill for many years so he used to bump into Joe all the time. He remembers Joe drinking several 'carajillos' (Spanish for coffee with Brandy) in the morning with the owner of a Spanish Cafe he had befriended. It was around the Clash II period and Joe was going through hell, **'he was looking depressed',** Mike said.

Mike believes Joe had it in him to be **'a Bruce Springsteen'** type of artist if he'd taken his solo career seriously instead of dabbling with acting and recording soundtracks. I agree.

When we talked about the last Clash line up he came up with a great line: **'you can't bring fans in expecting them to do what Mick Jones did!'** So true, and such a neat way of putting it.

Of course the man was right and history proves him right. Nick could play guitar for sure, Pete is a great drummer but too heavy for The Clash (**'he used to break skins often'** Fayne told me) specially if one compares Topper's finesse and subtlety with Pete's stomping energetic drumming, and then there's Vince.

Now I've been told that Vince could play guitar but I do have my doubts, I believe he was brought in because of his look (!) instead of his guitar skills. I'm aware that's not everyone's opinion, but it's been said Bernie was keen on hiring his services because he looked like a street Punk. Perhaps he also looked like a guy he could keep under his thumb for a while. **'He was a victim from day one,'** said Fayney about Vince. **'The others were cool. Pete and Nick are nice guys but Vince I didn't like. He was always moaning to me about Bernie and I wasn't saying anything because Bernie was cool with me. He gave me the job and he let me smoke weed while nobody else was allowed to. I guess Vince thought he could moan to me since I was neutral'.**

But Vince's guitar skills weren't precisely up to par with Nick's and his guitar actually *was* mixed down on the gigs, it wasn't Vince's paranoid delusions: **'I was told to make sure Nick's guitar was dominant in the mix, which isn't necessarily a bad thing!'** remembered Fayney.

Vince actually confesses in his book that it only during the Clash's last show, when he finally got his shit together, that he could play the whole repertoire without any bum notes. That doesn't say a lot about his technique. Also in his book Vince remembers Joe telling him how Pete and Nick didn't want him in the band because they thought he wasn't good enough to play in The Clash.

Now I've listened to a bunch of live bootlegs and Vince's guitar playing is nothing special and sometimes it sounds out of tune or time, in all fairness one could say he was an average guitar player at its best. Another proof of that is the two studio tracks they left behind: *Sex Mad Roar* and *Do It Now*, among the worst songs in the whole Clash catalogue along with 90 percent of *Cut the Crap*. Later I learned through Nick Sheppard that they only had one hour to record those two songs in Munich. That was the whole experience they had as a band in a proper recording studio: one hour.

The Weekend Festival at Laugharne in Wales was everything I could have hoped for. I met Johnny Green, Mick Jones, Robin Banks and other celebrities of the underworld such as Bruce Reynolds and Howard Marks. Topper missed the event because of the sudden passing of his mother but I had time to talk to Johnny and Robin and also a few minutes to make Mick understand the nature of my project.

I had met Mick a bunch of times before but of course he didn't remember. The first time was in 1990 when he came to Barcelona with 'BAD. II. It was one of their first ever shows and there I also met Nick Hawkins, the other guitar player in the band with whom I developed a friendship that lasted until his sudden death in 2005. In the early nineties I moved to London where I saw more of Nick and 'BAD. II as he would invite me to rehearsals, sound-checks and shows every now and then.

Mick listened to what I had to say and he encouraged me not only to go ahead and film his exhibition called The Mick Jones Public Rock & Roll Library at The Chelsea Space but to use whatever I wanted to because **'once you use it it's very hard to take it out'.**

Mick added I should talk to Vince and that he had read his book and couldn't believe his experience had been that horrible: **'it wasn't that bad when I was in the band'** said Jones.

It was getting late and we ended up talking about *Rude Boy* (**'we didn't like it at the time because it wasn't glamorous enough but now I'm happy we stuck with them'**), his show with Sid and Nancy in New York (**'we only did about six numbers, everybody was so out of it. But it was great to play with Arthur Kane, he was really a lovely guy'**), guitars (**'my favorite now is a Telecaster'**) and 'BAD.. When the chat was over Mick told me he'd think about my project and went back to the hotel where all of them were staying. I was staying in a cozy B&B with a strong smell of horse, the animal that is.

Back in London I started the first round of interviews with Subway Sect singer Vic Goddard, so we could have a chat about Bernie. Then it was Fayney, Barry 'Scratchy' Myers, Jock Scot, Pat Gilbert, Chris Salewicz, Vince White, Robin Banks, the

Blockheads' Mickey Gallagher, Norman Watt-Roy and finally Terry Chimes.

Terry showed up in a blue Mercedes Benz, it was one of those sports car for two passengers only but I forgot the model. He mentioned it on the phone but I'm not a car person, I like cars but I couldn't care less about the name of the model of that car or any other motor for that matter. Following Terry's expensive car into his gated residence I realized this guy had achieved what he had been after since the days of old. As legend has it, he was fired from The Clash because in one of Bernie's band meetings he mentioned he was in it to get a Lamborghini.

The interview was pretty good and Terry remembered his later experience with the band and the obvious tension that was building up between Mick and the rest of The Clash. Off camera, he remembered Joe stopping Mick from playing once: **'Mick was playing guitar with all the effects and Joe just put his hand on the strings to stop it. They didn't say anything but I remember Mick's face. I thought "Oh boy here we go!" Later Mick said to me: "did you see that?"'**.

The more I found out about The Clash the more I wondered how those guys managed to work together all those years and produce such great material with all that unspoken internal bullshit? Apparently The Clash were used to operating in that way - just like a **'dysfunctional family'** as Mick Jones puts it.

Jock Scot got involved with the band in the late seventies when he befriended Ian Dury in his native Scotland. He decided to move to London **'to look for these Punks because where I was from there wasn't any!'**. Sharing a flat with Kosmo, together with being in possession of a unique sense of humour, led to the Scotsman travelling with The Clash and becoming a familiar face in the their entourage.

During the interview Jock said something else that made me understand the whole picture a lot better, he remembered those days of '84 and '85 when there was a slight comeback of pseudo Punk Rock thanks to horrible bands like Anti Nowhere League and specially New Model Army; he reckons The Clash thought that by dyeing their hair orange, rehashing the line-up and toughening up the sound again they could step into that weak excuse for a 'movement' and keep the band going. That seems like a plausible theory for why The Clash tried to go back to 1977 in 1984. There's also Nick Sheppard's explanation: it was the easiest thing to do.

Vince's interview not only wasn't what I expected, but a lot worse. He showed up already pissed, wearing a pair of baggy white painter's trousers, a seventies shirt with a brown leather jacket, and a cheap pair of sunglasses. During the interview he kept repeating **'it's all in my book!'** as he didn't grasp the notion that I was filming him for a documentary and he had to explain it all for the camera...Forty minutes in, Vince started crying while remembering *This Is England* and that was the end of it.

A few days later I drove East to see The Blockheads play in the small town of Basildon. Fronted now by Derek the Draw, The Blockheads are still - thirty years after they started - one of the best bands in the UK and the interview I got with Mickey and Norman was just what I needed to complete another piece of the puzzle.

Norman painted a very sad picture of Joe in '85. According to his recollection, during the recording of *Cut the Crap* in Munich, Strummer had become a 'yes-man' to Bernie and was complying with all his orders. Paul wasn't there, **'it was just Joe'** said Norman. Even Robin Banks was shocked by some of the stuff he heard that night.

A few days later I met Eddie King and had a couple of beers with him in Camden Town, listening to his Clash stories. When I started talking about them keeping the brand alive for an extra two years after Mick's sacking, Eddie said, **'By 1982 The Clash were a multi-million dollar business'.** No wonder Bernie and Kosmo were adamant about carrying on with The Clash even after Joe had quit the band! Carry on Clash!

Eddie confirmed the bullying suffered by the new guys: **'we would all get it, one night it was Vince, another it was Nick, another night Pete got it... and I got it too!'.** He revealed that it was his brother and a girl whose name he had forgotten posing in the cover of *This Is England*; when I gave him a ride home he invited me in and got out the metal sheets he'd painted the original artwork for the *Straight To Hell* 12-inch onto. He told me he was looking for that rusty effect so he decided to paint it on metal and the truth is that both the cover and the dragon for the back cover still look amazing on that piece of steel.

Another person I met during my stay in London was Tracy Franks a long-time fan of The Clash who gave me some interesting clues about the story I was trying to piece together. She remembered being backstage at a show in Brixton Academy with Terry in '82; she said there was a real bad vibe and Mick wouldn't come out of the toilet for a good while. According to her, by that time they had lost it and it wasn't the same anymore.

Tracy also remembered that when the reconstituted, sans Mick Jones, line-up came to Brixton Academy on the 'The Clash Out Of Control Tour' in 1984, she altered the lettering announcing the gig outside the venue so that it read 'The Clash Con Tour'.

One Saturday night I ended up at a Rico Rodriguez show in Brixton with Tracy and Robin and there we met Chris Salewicz and The Specials' Jerry Dammers. Jerry expressed his wish to talk on film about Bernie Rhodes – the Specials had been managed by Bernie for a brief spell in 1979 and Dammers was more than familiar with the manager's peculiar ways. It was no coincidence that they dedicated their classic *Gangsters* to Rhodes.

For twenty days I chased as many interviews as I could and extended my list of potential contributors to around fifty instead of the initial thirty. When my budget started to run low, I decided to retreat and return to my base on the Costa Brava where I would mastermind my next excursion: Granada.

But before I left the British Isles I still had time to go up to Manchester and visit the art gallery that looks after the Ray Lowry estate these days. The owners of the See Gallery, Jackie and Julian, allowed me to film pages from the original sketch books Ray made while on tour with the Clash round America in 1979. The different styles that Lowry used on his work were truly mind blowing and the beauty of those three or four books really made me want to dedicate this project to him as well as to Joe and Nick Hawkins.

The material I got on tape is also a one-off because those sketch books will eventually be sold off, page by page. They're going already - at around £500 a page.

5. Spanish Bombs

Since the weekend in Wales I'd been friendly with Robin and he ended up coming over to Spain for a month, during which we had plenty of time to speak in depth about the project and the reality behind the scenes I had already shot. We spent a lot of time trying to figure out the truth, analyzing a bunch of other videos, interviews and different books and magazines.

One of the videos we watched a couple of times was the Roskilde '85 bootleg where Paul can be seen like you've never seen him on stage before: running around throwing shapes, breakdancing and even singing *What's My Name?* without a bass or guitar in his hands. **'I never saw Paul looking uncool before!'** Robin concluded after seeing the show. It looked like without Mick and Topper, Paul was now King of the stage next to Joe, and had taken to playing the Court jester.

Watching Roskilde '85 you realize that what Vince talks about in his book is probably all true, especially his assessment that **'what was once a lean tight hungry outfit was now a lumbering giant. A big fat cat slowly gorging its way through all the stadiums of the USA.'** Watching that show you also realize that in 1985 The Clash were no longer relevant, at least not that Clash anyway. The way I see it, Clash II were the ultimate Clash cover band, and that's for sure.

Topper was calling Robin all the time so I had the chance to say hello to him on the blower a couple of times, he sounded cheerful and glad Robin was enjoying himself under the Spanish Sun.

Robin also spoke to Tymon Dogg who was spending the summer in San Jose, a small town by the sea near Almería, about an hour from Granada, and a holiday destination for Joe and his family since the 1980s. Tymon sounded interested in the documentary and when Robin told him how surprised he was about the influence Bernie had on Joe at the end of The Clash, Tymon just said: **'he was always looking for that father figure, wasn't he?'**.

Meanwhile I had arranged to meet some of Joe's friends in Granada: Music journalist Jesús Arias, 101ers and PIL drummer Richard Dudanski, and a couple of the guys from 091, the local band that Joe produced in 1985.

Crossing the Almeria desert I thought about *Straight To Hell*, the Alex Cox film Joe starred in along with The Pogues, Elvis Costello and Courtney Love in 1986. I tried to imagine the fun these guys must have had in this baking hot corner of Spain.

The first thing we did when we got to Granada was shoot the magnificent Alhambra from the very same spot where Joe had posed in October of 1984 - el Mirador de San Nicolás. Nowadays it's usually crowded with tourists, hippies selling their merchandise and gypsies singing and playing flamenco guitar.

According Jesús Arias, Joe went to Granada **'to suffer the pain for his mistakes'** and the first thing he said to Jesús upon learning his name was: **'Please forgive me!'**. Aside from being typical of Joe's sense of humour, it also suggests that just one year later, Joe was repenting for firing Topper and Mick and to all intents and purposes destroying the band he loved so much.

But before I interviewed Jesús in Granada we met Tymon in San José for one of the best interviews I had done for the documentary so far. Tymon showed up wearing a straw hat and a smile that crossed his face from side to side. The man looked extremely good for his age, perhaps the fact that he is a vegan – **'I don't eat anything with a face!'** - has something or everything to do with his healthy aspect. Over an early afternoon Spanish beer, Tymon spoke openly about Joe, The Mescaleros, Bernie and a lost album he did in 1983 which Joe produced. Called *Hollowed Out* it is now a poignant homage-in-waiting to their long friendship and was engineered by the legendary Glyn Johns: **'Joe plays on a few tracks. I have the master tapes but it has to be mixed,'** Tymon revealed.

After the drinks we headed for the beaches to try to find a quiet spot where I could interview Mr Dogg. We explored the surroundings of San José and admired the beauty of the Cabo de Gata national park. No wonder Joe loved it there, it is a truly unique and timeless landscape which wouldn't look amiss in 'Jurassic Park'. We set up the camera and tried to shoot under the shelter of some rocks but the sound of the wind and the breaking of the waves made it impossible to work there.

On the way back to the car we spoke about songwriters, politricks and obviously about Joe...'**I taught him how to play guitar – seems like I do that with everybody who's around** me... I think everybody has at the very least two or three good songs in them...! Joe and I spent a lot of time together for five years or so, he was trying to learn the mystery of music. Because music was very mysterious to him you know? Joe was not a musical guy and it took him a long time to come up with his first song but he wrote some great stuff after'.

Tymon suggested we could go back to the house he was renting to film the interview so we headed back to San José. After the cameras were off, as often happens, the interviewee kept talking about things related to the story. Tymon remembered meeting Bernie Rhodes not too long ago and during their conversation apparently something extraordinary had occurred: Bernie apologized for everything! 'I didn't mean to hurt anyone,' Rhodes allegedly told Tymon referring to the whole Clash trip, and showing some kind of repentance for his actions. I couldn't believe my ears... shame I didn't get that on film!

The next day we were back in Granada looking for Jesús. He'd met Joe a few days after he had landed in Federico García Lorca's city, probably looking for some peace of mind and a bit of inspiration to help him write the final material for *Cut the Crap*. Quickly Jesús became Joe's translator and go between. 091, the local band he loved so much, and the locals in general, couldn't believe Strummer was hanging out with them enjoying Granada's finest beer, rather predictably labeled *Alhambra*.

One of Joe's favourite bars was La Sabanilla, an old joint from 1883 where Lorca was supposed to have been a regular. During an interview Jesús asked Joe what Lorca meant to him and Strummer replied: **'Lorca is that empty chair at La Sabanilla'**...Robin and I ended up visiting the little bar and took a few shots of the place, drank some of their sweet wine, ate some of their tapas and when we asked for the bill they told us it was free for us and that we should thank Lorca for it! Robin suggested we should thank Joe for it as well and that we did shouting **'Thank you Joe'** as we walked back to the square where we were to meet up with Richard 'Snakehips' Dudanski.

Richard showed up smiling and happy to meet us in a bodega in the part of town where he resides. He soon made it clear that he didn't want to be interviewed for the documentary because he didn't have anything to add to it, not having been in the loop during those last Clash years.

Dudanski did remember a legendary 1976 Bernie episode in the 101'ers squat however: **'I came down one morning and there's this guy in the living room talking to Joe and Mickey Foote, who was the 101'ers manager, and I said "no way, not with this guy!"'** Apparently Richard saw right away that Bernie meant trouble and took an instant dislike to the soon to be Clash manager. If it hadn't been for Bernie, Richard might have taken up the offer to be the Clash's drummer.

After another quick drink we left Dudanski in the company of his wife Esperanza, sister of Palmolive of The Slits, and disappeared into the night. Driving back I noticed the sign for Viznar, the place where Lorca was shot and buried by fascists and where almost fifty years later Joe had smoked a joint in the memory of the assassinated poet under the shade of an olive tree.

6. Groovy Times

Back in London in mid-July I hopped in a cab and headed directly to Notting Hill. Three days before my arrival Mick Jones had opened his Public Rock & Roll Library in number 2 Acklam Road, on the corner with Portobello and literally beneath the Westway and that was where I was going. 'It doesn't get more Clash than that,' I thought to myself.

Robin greeted me at the door and we walked upstairs to where Mick, Chris Salewicz and others were enjoying a drink after a hard day's work. I had a look around and admired the exhibition while Mr. Jones walked around rearranging his books and things, improving his installation. Something he'd do every day for the next two weeks.

This time the Library had been installed in a location that was at least ten times bigger than its previous home at The Chelsea Space. Here there was a main hall with some of Mick's books, clothes, toys, gold and platinum records, vinyls, classic Fender amplifiers and different sorts of memorabilia plus a few smaller rooms to help display his huge magazine collection, VHS tapes and even a small cinema where *Westway to the World* could be seen every day from 11 to 7pm.

At the other end of the premises Mick had set up a small recording studio with a live room in collaboration with Strummerville (a charity in memory of Joe) where young bands would record their demos every other day, some of them produced by Mick. Appropriately enough the live room was called Strummer while the control room was named Jones.

For the next month I became a fixture in the building, spending as much time as possible there, especially at night. Mick was there every night hanging out and as the nights rolled by we ended up having pretty interesting conversations ranging from history to cinema, art, politics, etc. I had to leave The Clash questions out of the equation unless it was related to a particular item displayed in the Library in which case Mick would gladly explain the history behind any piece of the exhibition.

I was fascinated by a collection of pictures that hung on the walls of the green room, where we would be sitting around every night. They revealed a particular Clash story that I never heard about before. It was a bunch of photographs dating back to '78 when The Clash played a game of football with some kids in Camden Town. Some guy who knew Mick and used to coach kids in the neighborhood invited the band to play with the boys and of course...they accepted. It was the four of them plus Johnny Green, Ray Gange and some other roadies. Topper and Simonon were wearing sneakers but Joe played the game in his leather boots.

It was just a small story but I thought that was **'a Clash thing to do'**. One of the first things Mick told me was that I had arrived at the right moment and that I would meet **'lots of interesting people'** who would be useful for my documentary. I knew what he was talking about but I didn't expect to get to know such an amazing bunch of people related to Mick's musical career.

The second day I was there I met Leo 'E-Z Kill' Williams, the BAD, Dreadzone and Carbon/Silicon bass player with whom I spoke briefly about his days with the Top Risk Action Company (TRAC) that Mick had formed with Topper immediately after leaving the Clash. I'd seen a photograph of them in one of Mick's books and Leo said the outfit didn't last long: Topper **'was too**

sick to play' and the sound was **'too much like The Clash'** as far as Leo was concerned.

Dan Donovan was another BAD member I ran into a few times. I interviewed him briefly for the documentary, talking about the Bahamas incident of 1985 when Joe went out there looking for Mick desperately trying to put back the band together again. One of those *Spinal Tap* moments of The Clash's history according to Jones himself. Gary Stonadge (bass player in 'BAD II) told me later that before the Nassau incident Strummer had been hanging around the studio where Mick would be, trying to talk him into getting the real Clash back together.

A couple of times Mick asked me how the project was coming along showing his interest and gladly allowed me to shoot any interviews I wished on the premises. But even though Robin was now fully involved in the process of the making of the film, Mick was still unsure about giving us the interview and kept postponing, much to our despair. Robin kept telling me, **'Don't worry, he'll do it'** and although I truly trusted his words I had my doubts – quite reasonably, given the nature of the documentary.

The first interview I did on this leg of the operation was with music journalist, Kris Needs. Although Kris had been in many Clash-related documentaries before, he had witnessed the whole thing and I was sure he'd have many relevant things to say, plus I liked his commentaries and his humble Keef kind of approach to life. His interview turned out to be one of the funniest we'd done for this project, especially when he remembered Paul Simonon building up salads on Bernie's shoulders as the manager spoke to the press or the mural Paul painted which was simply called 'Bernie is Odd'.

The other interview I had lined up was with Mark Helfond. Mark posed as 'the Jew' for the cover of the *Rock The Casbah* single and was the Bernie's helper in the '82 - '83 period. Unfortunately that interview didn't go so well. Helfond aka Frothler, turned out to be very defensive of Bernie's interests and didn't reveal much at all except when the cameras weren't rolling, then he told me **'the real reason for sacking Topper wasn't what you are thinking. There was something else but I can't tell you, it's too embarrassing. You should ask them'**. I was surprised to hear that because like everyone else I always believed Topper was fired because of his addiction to opiates. Robin didn't even know what Frothler was on about and we forgot all about it.

On Sunday July 26th we attended a historic event at the legendary 100 Club in Oxford Street. It was a benefit show for author Terry Rawlings who was suffering from cancer and Mick would be playing a few numbers along with fellow Punk Rock stars Glen Matlock and Steve Diggle to help raise funds towards Rawlings' hospital bill.

We were already familiar with the set list because Glen had been up in the Library rehearsing with Jones the previous week and we'd heard them playing *Should I Stay Or Should I Go*, *Train In Vain*, *Pretty Vacant*, *Stepping Stone* and *You Really Got Me*. What we didn't expect was to witness a unique event in R&R history when the spirit of '76 came back to the 100 Club with members of the Sex Pistols, The Clash and The Buzzcocks playing on stage together for the first time.

The place was packed and the crowd reacted energetically to the Punk super-group re-enacting the pogo that Sid invented back then. As the music hit me I remember how I'd loved those songs as a kid and I realized why I'm a music fan in the first place. It was that energy that got me.

When it was time for *You Really Got Me* the trio were joined by The Kinks' drummer Mike Avery and as the final chord was struck the show was over. After the gig, Mick was ecstatic and in the midst of it all he agreed to do the interview the next day at six in the Library. I was over the moon, not only I had seen an amazing show but Mick had said 'yes' to the project. Things couldn't get better.

Come Monday at six we were ready to shoot when Mick announced he wasn't doing it. He was pacing around the room talking to me and saying stuff like, **'We didn't like each other anymore! Those things happen in bands!'** and going back to Robin to ask him, **'Why should I do it? You know you are not going to get Paul! And you know you are not going to get Bernie!'.**

I was petrified and couldn't muster a word at first, then I started agreeing with Mick, burbling that he didn't need to do anything, he'd said it all before. Robin looked at me and told me to, **'Shut up'** and to stop encouraging him not to do it. For the first time since I'd started on this endeavor I was working against my own interests just out of respect for the man. Tony James was there in another room and after a few minutes he and Mick left the building for a couple of hours with the promise that he'd think about it yet again. **'Don't worry, he'll do it'**, Robin repeated his mantra for the hundredth time.

I had to admire Banks' perseverance and his gentle way of working Mick, making him understand the importance of his presence in the film. Having Jones on board would make the world of a difference and Robin knew that more than anybody. A lifelong friendship was what Banksy relied on and he wasn't wrong because as soon as Mick came back he gave us the final **'OK'** and at last we were rolling.

Mick's interview went down really well. I had come up with a short, sharp questionnaire in order not to abuse Jonesy's good grace and hospitality. Mick responded to the questions very solemnly and truthfully as well as very fast and soon I was scratching my head searching for more questions to ask the man. I couldn't screw the only chance I had to interview Jones so I started going through the questions I'd asked before, trying to stick to the program.

I had to think fast and I managed to pull a few extra questions together without repeating myself too much. We ended up with a half hour piece where Mick relived some of the worst moments he had experienced with the band he helped create back in '76. He spoke openly about the drug problems in the group, Bernie and his tactics, Terry, Tops, Paul and gave us the final word on the subject.

According to Robin, **'That's the last time he'll speak on camera about The Clash'**.

The morning after, still high from the Jonesy interview, Robin decided to call Bernie and engaged with him in what seemed an amicable conversation for almost an hour trying to convince him to join us and speak for once about his times with The Clash. **'You have to do it sometime Bernie!'** Robin kept saying. When the call was over he told me **'he wants to speak to you, call him back in ten minutes'**.

Soon I was talking again with the mystery man. This time around his tone was different, he no longer sounded like an inquisitive and defensive man but rather relaxed.

Suddenly he started going on about how The Clash had got rid of him in the first place. I told him I'd heard he wasn't communicating with them, messing around with their wages, and so on... as soon as Johnny Green's name came up he called him **'an impostor'** and referred to his background (surprise, surprise!) as something he couldn't trust. **'But you didn't care about Joe's background when you asked him to join the band!'** I replied, disgusted by Bernie's classism and in defense of Johnny, someone who I admire for his work as well as his sense of humor and who I owe for hooking me up with Mick.

I passed the phone back to Robin and he was soon shouting things like **'Bernie! don't talk like that about Johnny! He's one of my best friends!'** There was nothing doing with Mr. Rhodes and it soon became clear that what Mark Helfond told me was 100% accurate: **'Bernie will never agree to talk about The Clash on camera'**.

That evening Mick was recording a song up in the Library with Gaz Mayall and an array of Notting Hill acolytes as a tribute to Great Train Robber legend Ronnie Biggs, still in custody and suffering from pneumonia in a Norwich hospital at that point.
By the time we got there, the Strummer and Jones rooms of the Library were already in full swing. The track ended up being nothing more than a jam but the lyrics in the chorus were kind of funny. I remember when Mick sung it for us days before they recorded it: **'Ronnie Biggs should be knighted, Ronnie Biggs should be delighted. With his get out of jail free card, getting out shouldn't be so hard'**.

As the days rolled by I also met filmmaker and BAD founding member Don Letts with whom I spoke about the possibility of having some of his Clash archive on my film. Although he refused to be interviewed for the documentary, Don was cool about it and we decided to meet another day when we could watch his collection of super-8 footage dating back to 1976.

Don's stepbrother, Desmond Coy, was running the Library during the day and we had some interesting conversations about the beginnings of BAD. Desmond used to road manage them until he got fired for taking his job too seriously. He was in charge of the party department and apparently they were partying too hard given Des' expertise in that particular field.

One Wednesday night we were relaxing in the Green Room when Damon Albarn and another guy showed up. Damon was really drunk and left a few seconds after walking into the Library and saying: **'what is this?'**. Just when we were wondering what the fuck was going on, Paul Simonon showed up with Mick and a couple of guys. Apparently they had left a Gorillaz session and decided to pop in for a private view of the exhibition.

I shook hands with Paul and reminded him about the time I interviewed him in Barcelona back in 91. **'That's a long time ago!'** he said smiling, and after small talk disappeared into the main hall with the others to enjoy Mick's installation.

An hour later Paul was getting ready to leave; I knew I had to seize my opportunity and ask him if he'd like to be part of the documentary. I pitched the project like my life depended on it and then he said: **'Look, the best way to put it... it's like a rocket. You light it, it goes up, it frizzles a bit, explodes, lands on the floor... and there you are!'**.

Wow! That was so cool that I immediately framed him with my fingers from the distance like movie directors do and I said: 'If I could get that on camera that would be amazing!' Paul said, **'Okay, well call me tomorrow and we'll see what we can do about it'**. We exchanged numbers and moments later I watched him disappear into the night on his bike heading towards Ladbroke Grove. I called Robin right away and gave him the news, he couldn't believe his ears specially since he was the one who'd recently told me: **'forget about Paul, getting him would be a miracle'.**

But Robin wasn't wrong after all, and two days later Paul backed off, telling me that basically he, **'Didn't feel like talking about the end of The Clash'.** Robin tried to convince him otherwise but got nowhere and that was that.

Don and Paul wouldn't be the only ones to say 'no' to the interviews while I was in London. The list also included Alex Michon, Pete Townshend, Topper Headon and Johnny Green. The reason we didn't get Johnny was because he was away on holiday somewhere in France. That was a real shame because, according to Robin, he was **'ready to spill the beans'.** I wondered if I'd still have another chance to film him and Topper answering some questions together as Robin had suggested months earlier. Que será...

Even though the list of casualties was growing alarmingly fast there was still one veteran I had to question and that was none other than Pete Howard, the last drummer to play with The Clash and a key witness to the whole decline of the band.

Arranging Pete's interview was never easy from the start and this time around wasn't going to be different but we finally got around to do it on a Saturday afternoon. We met at his house near Finsbury Park, not far from Blackstock Road, where the last line up of The Clash ended up rehearsing once Bernie had lost Rehearsals in 1985.

The interview lasted over an hour and twenty minutes and it would be the longest I had done for this project. Pete was easy to interview and gave lengthy answers about the way the band ended. At some point he told me my questions were too focused on the negative aspect of the whole story so Pete started mentioning the good times which were mainly to do with the countries he'd visited and the people he had met along the way. There were no tales of Rock life's excesses or greatness to tell on his part. No gold records or huge amounts of money to show for his job in one of the biggest bands the UK has ever exported.

He had to agree with me that the period he was in the band hadn't been easy and that was why the tone of the questions weren't exactly cheerful. He confessed the experience in The Clash had damaged him personally, perhaps not as much as it did Vince, but maybe halfway there.

Back in the Library, the Dan Donovan interview took place and even though it was the shortest we did for the whole project it was actually really good. Dan remembered finding a pissed Joe mucking about in the swimming pool when he arrived in the villa Mick was staying in in Nassau. But basically **'it was too late'** to get The Clash back on track. Dan returned to London on a flight with Joe and he was still pissed, apparently he'd managed to stay drunk on Rum the whole two or three days they spent together in the Bahamas.

A few days after that I went to the Inn on the Green to catch Viv Albertine doing a low key show. Mark Perry's Alternative TV were also on the bill and I watched them from the back of the room with Ray Gange for a while. **'Thinking man's Punk'** said Ray referring to Mark P's band which I'd never seen before.

After the gig I spoke to Viv and she offered to be interviewed for the project. **'I knew Bernie,'** she said. **'He used to treat me really bad'**.

Joe's friend Pockets was also present that night at the Inn. I'd met him before when he'd just returned from Japan where he was representing the charity organization set up in Joe's memory, Strummerville, at the Fuji Rock Festival. As a trustee, Pockets helps carry on the torch at street level; helping out the bands recording at Mick's Library, sorting out rehearsals for artists and basically doing anything that takes to make sure Strummerville is there doing its thing. Robin told me how Joe met Pockets when he was basically living in the street and ended up taking him up to Somerset where he lived for years even after Joe's passing.

A while later I met Don at the Library again so we could watch his Punk archive. It was a three hour VHS tape and the fast forward wasn't working which meant I had to sit tight and go through the whole three hours making notes of what interested me. Don left me in the screening room and I started taking in it all in. You don't get to watch Don's archive everyday so I wanted to make sure I got hold of the best I could get. The footage for the Punk Rock Movie was all over, also stuff used by Julien Temple, Alan G. Parker and Letts himself in *Westway to the World*. But as Don told me there was plenty of it that's never been released yet.

Don's Punk archive included Clash shows from '76 to '79 and were filmed on Super-8. The early stuff was pretty messy and sometimes out of focus but as the years rolled by Letts's technique got better and better and soon I was watching excellent bits of shows from the White Riot tour and finally a show with Mickey Gallagher and Mickey Dread sharing the stage with the band.

The next day Don introduced me to Julien Temple who happened to show up at the Library and I spoke with him briefly about the early footage he owns of The Clash. He told me about a video they did for *London's Burning* where due to the low budget they burned postcards of London. **'That's Punk!'** Don said.

Spending a month in Portobello in the summertime proved to be a total Clash experience that any fan should live at least once. Walking past Joe's house in Lancaster Road almost daily reminded me of my purpose and made me even more aware of the task that was in my hands. So far it had been a unique thing and I always did my best to get as many people involved and tried to extract as much information as I could from every single source. Even people in the neighborhood, like Tony, the Liverpudlian that runs *Hideout,* a clothing store in Portobello. Tony has known Nick Sheppard since the early 80's and amongst other things he told me how Nick was **'devastated when The Clash broke up'**.

It was pretty amazing being able to discuss anything Clash with the man running the corner store. Mick's exhibition brought a lot of life to Portobello attracting tourists, locals and fans who travelled miles to get to see Jones' collection. The funny thing about it is that **'that's only the tip of the iceberg'** - talking to Mick about it I suggested that given the volume of memorabilia he's got, he could have four exhibitions like that one in four different places round the World all at the same time and he agreed that that was actually a fact.

But there was something quite remarkable about that small balcony overlooking Portobello Market where we would all spend vast amounts of time smoking, drinking and watching life go on in

Portobello Road, listening to the sounds of Dub vendors selling their CDs to the punters every weekend. You couldn't miss the fact that that was what inspired Paul, Joe, Mick and Topper in the first place. No wonder they felt so proud to be part of that urban landscape. Notting Hill, Portobello, Ladbroke Grove, the Westway...W10 had become my home for four weeks and I was sure I would miss the place and its people but it was time to face the music and I did.

7. Long Time Lapse

The following months were mostly boring and slow as I dedicated my efforts to negotiating with footage owners, music publishers, photographers and record companies trying to get as much material as possible before we started editing.

I was pursuing an interview with Ellen Foley, convinced that she would have a few interesting things to say about the band but once I sent her the questionnaire she just said she had forgotten most of it and wouldn't be of any help.

I needed to get at least one woman to agree to be in the film, I'd had no luck trying to reach the great photographer Pennie Smith, Viv Albertine offered to be in it but for now I'd lost contact with her and now Ellen didn't seem to recall much from her experience with The Clash. But suddenly it hit me, of course! I should contact Pearl Harbor! The R&R singer and Simonon's first wife. She of course was a witness to the rise and fall of the group and travelled around the World with them a few times.

I remembered Chris Salewicz giving me Rudy Fernandez's phone number and telling me to contact him and ask about Pearl because he would have her number. So I called Rudy and I was glad to find out that he was another great guy willing to help out a fellow Clash fan. He told me he'd ask Pearl if she'd be interested in giving me an interview and that's how it happened.

Next day Rudy confirmed her interest and passed me her number so we could arrange it. I wasn't gonna be able to travel to L.A so one of my contributors, Andrew Matey from San Francisco would be in charge of those interviews.

Pearl turned out to be practically the missing link in the story. She sounded really interested in the documentary and also very truthful as she remembered the division of camps within the group. **'I belonged to the Strummer camp'** she said and assured me she didn't want to talk negative stuff about anybody. I told her she could say whatever she wanted and the mere fact that she was acknowledging the existence of two camps in the band was already new information.

As the weeks rolled by I also got another long-distance interview done. Finally Mr. Nick Sheppard had agreed to do an interview for the film and, from his home in Perth, offered us another missing piece of the puzzle we were trying to put together.

Nick's interview was so sincere and revealing I wanted to share it with others. I told Robin straight away, and Johnny Green, and even Mick, who wasn't impressed by my findings. Wait 'til you hear the rest of it I thought to myself, I didn't want to bore him with the rest of it.

My relationship with Bernie suffered a bit through this period. First it was the interview I sent him by email which he took offense at; although they were a bunch of sincere questions, the tone was too cheeky for him.

After a bit of email turbulence with Mr Rhodes, I kept pushing the Pearl interview and negotiating licensing deals with various sources. Also, the script started to come together once the transcripts of the interviews were done. The material was clearly great.

Other people I got in touch around this period were Ray Jordan who agreed to talk to me when I returned to London; Mickey Foote, who also said he'd like to have a chat; Chris Townsend (the man behind 5th Column, makers of The Clash original tour T-shirts) and Hermann Weindorf from Weryton Studios, Munich, where the band recorded most of *Cut the Crap*. Hermann (credited in CTC as Young Wagner) was responsible for the keyboards in that album, not Mickey Gallagher as it was widely rumoured. I spoke to Hermann about visiting Weryton with a cameraman exactly 25 years after Joe and Bernie showed up with a few guys trying to make history. They did in fact make history, but perhaps for all the wrong reasons. Hermann agreed in principle but claimed he didn't have much to say because he **'only worked with them for three days'** during which he'd be asking Bernie what he wanted him to do and **'there was no answer'**...

Perhaps Hermann did believe he didn't have much to tell but I thought the things he said were brilliant! Yet another piece of the puzzle was emerging, even if it was a little one, Hermann and his studios in Munich were definitely worth a visit.

The engineer that worked with The Clash at Weryton was Ulrich Rudolf, known as Uli. Apparently Uli told Hermann the band had been fighting in the studio, arguing... obviously struggling to come up with some half decent sounds.

Pearl's interview turned out to be probably the best one in the whole collection. She spoke so honestly and when she explained everything made it sound so simple and obvious that my detective work suddenly seemed a bit superfluous.

Around this time I decided to email Bernie again and apologize for having said all that ugly stuff to him. I had a few reasons for this. Even though he had started our e-beef, for some reason I thought that apologizing might not be his forte so I decided I would apologize instead. Bernard responded like he was glad that I did and we resumed our relationship like nothing had ever happened.

I also spoke to Mickey Foote a couple of times on the phone. He sounded like he was another one of these extremely nice people that floated around The Clash camp. We spoke about the demos he did with the band before the first album came out, a bit about *Combat Rock*: **'it was nice to be in the studio with them again'** he said, and of course: Bernie. He and Mr. Rhodes had parted ways in a stormy fashion once The Clash ship sunk after the *Cut the Crap* debacle. Apparently Bernard pestered Mickey to side with him in a possible Court case where he would demand The Clash the money he was owed for his services. Foote wouldn't take the phone and avoided the situation. After all, he had been friends with Joe since the squat days and manager of The 101'ers before producing The Clash's first album and then becoming Bernard's right hand man for years. Bernie finally settled out of

Court with the band and Mickey has never spoken to Rhodes since.

When the time seemed right and I finally got around to phoning Bernie again, I confronted him cautiously with some new revelations I'd got from Pearl.

Bernie started talking about drum machines, saying Joe decided to start using them because **'he wanted to compete with Mick Jones' drum machine thing'**. Moving onto *Cut the Crap*, he said **'it's not *that* bad'**…I'd been expecting him to defend it, saying it was great or groundbreaking but no, just 'not *that* bad.'

I also mentioned the fact that Pearl had heard him discuss sacking Mick with Joe and Paul way before it actually happened; now he admitted it: **'with one foot we were trying to keep him in the band and with the other foot we were trying to kick him out!'** Wow! I couldn't believe it! Probably for the first time in 25 years Bernie recognized his involvement in the sacking of Mick.

He also mentioned that Joe hadn't wanted to use the new guys on the new record and the fact that Joe was a **'nice bloke but very traditional, you know?'.**

I told him that my conclusion on the whole Clash thing, after studying it in depth for more than a year, was that the band's ultimate goal was simply to inspire people. **'That's it!!'** he shouted. I had never heard him sound so excited… it made me feel as if I was the first to decipher that one in 30 years!

Before I travelled one last time to London to resume shooting I gave Paul Simonon a call in a last attempt to get him to collaborate with us and allow me to interview him for five minutes. Basically my message was: I've spoken to Pearl, she has explained everything very clearly and in such a simple way that a three year old could understand it and there's nothing to hide or be ashamed of. But there was nothing doing. **'I'm more interested in what I'm doing tomorrow than in what I did yesterday.** said Paul. But even he had to admit that it **'sounds like you got something'** referring to the contents of the documentary and that he'd like **'to watch it on the screen'** once it's done. I thanked him again and promised to be in touch. One thing must be said on his behalf and that is that Paul is always a gentleman.

8. London Calling

On 7 January 2010 I was back in London to get the last interviews in the can before we started editing. Before flying to London I had finally arranged to interview Viv Albertine, Ray Jordan and Chris Townsend plus I was going to try to get Ray Gange, Mickey Foote, Jerry Dammers and Peter Jenner to talk to us on camera.

Robin tried and tried again with Topper but after the drummer saw the script he declined to be interviewed, saying something about **'dragging over old coals'.** Johnny Green wasn't sure about his contribution either and we left it at that.

I can understand Topper not wanting to talk about bad stuff, if I was in his shoes I'd probably take the same view. But nevertheless there seems to be some kind of sworn secrecy around things related to the band that past 25 or 30 years I wouldn't have expected to be taboo anymore. **'It was about honesty, wasn't it?'** said Johnny Green to me once, and he was right of course. Shame you didn't spill the beans this time around Mr Green.

The final interviews took place upstairs at Map Studio Café, the place Chris Townsend owns in Kentish Town. A great place to eat, drink, buy records and watch live bands of an evening.

A few of the interviewees fell through but we managed to shoot Viv Albertine at last. She was brilliant on and off camera, even directing me while I was interviewing her, **'move a bit to the right'** she'd say to make sure she was looking at the right place when she would respond.

Before the interview she told us that it was she who told Mick not to write any more love songs, because that's what Mick was doing when they met in Art School. She said *Train In Vain* is dedicated to her, **'their best song,'** she added.

The previous night David Mingay told me about a huge row he had witnessed back in '78 between Viv and Mick in a parking lot somewhere in the UK. She was chasing him around kicking him in the balls and in the ass. She laughed when I told her about it. Apparently that wasn't completely unusual during their explosive relationship and Robin added a little story about another fight during the White Riot tour in 1977… The Clash and The Slits were staying in some hotel and Mick and Viv were having one of their fights when suddenly Mick found himself under attack from all four Slits. Robin went charging down the corridor to the rescue while the Slits ran back to their rooms, locking their doors and leaving Jones to live another day.

Eddie King came down to the Café too, but just to see us and some of his old friends. He repeatedly declined – in the kindest possible way - to be interviewed but later he took me round to 5th Column where Soj gave me three of the original tee shirts that they used to sell with The Clash on the American tours of 1979 and 1982.

Eddie always had great Clash stories to tell and that's why it was so painful not being able to interview him. At some point he said: **'if Kosmo does it, I'll do it'**. He knew Kosmo wasn't doing it so that was it.

One of the interesting tit-bits he mentioned concerned some dog tags they had ready to manufacture back in 1984. One of them read 'The Clash' and the other 'Out Of Control'. Reason being that at that point Mick had had all the assets frozen and there were rumblings about the ownership of the name of the group… in the event of losing the name they had resolved to call themselves 'Out Of Control'. This is why, during those last two years, the tours were called 'Out Of Control'.

Ray Jordan finally showed up and gave probably his first interview for a Clash related project ever. He had witnessed it all from 1979 to 1985 from the privileged perspective of being the band's body guard. His sense of humor and his excellent memory offered us yet another piece of the puzzle that helped us to see the big picture a lot better.

After the interview he told me that once the band was over Joe had said to him: **'I guess now you're gonna write a book about me, huh?'** but Ray replied **'no, I won't'** because if he did he could tell a lot of stuff that nobody's ever read…**'I know everything!'** he added with a chuckle.

Foote, Gange, Dammers and Jenner couldn't make it so we ended up asking David Mingay to sit down and respond to a few questions. The funniest bit of his interview was when he remembered visiting Bernie in his flat. The manager took him to an empty room with two piles of *Marxism Today*, which Bernie used as chairs. I thought that was genius! How could the man be a fake when he was using a bunch of communist magazines to sit on?

When I told Eddie King I thought Bernie was a cool guy, he said **'it's called Bernarditis, don't worry you'll be alright'** and patted me on the back.

I thought that was funny, but maybe he was right and I had been Bernified over the last twelve months. The truth is, I think Bernie is a very creative man… didn't Joe say that? And I totally understand why Joe and Paul dug his thinking and his ideas. Pearl told me he was also **'a great male ego booster'** and I knew what she meant by that when I finally met Bernard. He will say stuff to make you see the big picture and to make you feel like you're either important or you could be important if you only listen to what he's got to say.

Having been told so much about Bernie, good and bad, plus all the times we'd spoken, I had begun to understand what he was about when I finally got the chance to see him face to face.

We met in Richmond and ended up spending over four hours walking around, going to bookstores and art galleries, having a bite and drinking a couple of beers and vodka shots. We spoke about ideas and projects I had on my mind and my impression is that Bernie is very relaxed these days and still has it in him to do something in the music business, maybe not for the money but just for the sake of it. At least that was my impression. He also told me once that when he starts a project it's **'all work, work, work'**, something I had been told beforehand and which I understood given the limited lifespan of groups. **'You have to stop thinking like the Rolling Stones!'** Bernie said to me once when he mentioned starting up a number of projects rather than just one.

One of the only Clash-related conversations we had was while we were having drinks at a place appropriately called Revolution. *Rock The Casbah* came on the speakers and I asked him if he knew that was a hit from the first moment. He said yes and that he **'didn't know Topper had written it'**. He added that Mick didn't like it at first, something I had read before and that probably has to do with the fact that he didn't write it. Bernard went on to say that **'people say I don't like Topper'** but that it was he who pushed for that song to be finished.

A great Bernard anecdote that Eddie King told me happened during the last American tour. All the road crew were lined up ready to start the tour when Bernie shows up and yells at them: **'I only have one thing to say to you: Rock & Roll is dead!'** And walks off.

It was easy to understand why Joe and Paul wanted Bernie to manage them. There aren't many Bernie Rhodes around in the music industry!

At this point I understood that while I may have developed a soft spot for Bernard, it was still an objective fact that blaming it all on him was way too simplistic.

Ray Jordan had confirmed how hard it had been to cope with Topper's drug addiction and Mick's Rock Star lifestyle on the road; how both of them had brought conflict with the band upon themselves and hadn't made things any easier for the rest.

Pearl had told us that while Joe, Paul, Kosmo and Bernie were on the same trip, Mick was a different type of guy. Terry acknowledged the increasing tensions and saw the end coming way before it actually happened.

Pete, Vince and Nick told us about the last years of the band and yes, what a shitty end for a great band...

But we're still talking about them now, after all these years and that is because of the great music they left behind... a legacy that matters so much more than the legend, the paradoxes and all the rest of it.

It is truly magnificent.

Shooting The Clash

Mike Laye remembers the day he got a call from Clash manager, Bernie Rhodes, saying, 'Can you keep a secret? We've sacked Mick and we need to do a photo shoot for the press.'

Mike had known The Clash since 1976; he promoted the second and third gigs they ever did as Director of the ICA Theatre in London and worked with Bernie Rhodes at Rehearsal Rehearsals for a while, before finally settling into a career as a photographer.

Now he was being asked to photograph a version of The Clash that numbered just Paul and Joe. He recalls that, while Paul was his usual straight-forward, positive self, Joe was edgy, tired and stressed that day.

Mike kept the secret, as promised: 'One of the best kept secrets in Rock and Roll, as it turns out – and for four whole weeks!'

Soon he was asked do two more sessions with the newly recruited replacement band members. 'I found it really disquieting,' he says. 'Partly, I felt sort of disloyal to Mick, but I also got this feeling that Joe was being somehow manipulated, he seemed distant, not the Joe I knew.'

In retrospect Mike believes that Strummer was suffering real torment and mental anguish. 'I should have said, come on Joe, leave it, you've done your bit, it's over, let's get out of here ... I should have, but ... we just got on with the job.'

The photos in this book are from the 'secret shoot' and the two subsequent sessions. They have never been published before.

Joe Streno recalls how, as a young photographer working on a shoe-string, he got his first break thanks to the Clash: 'Back in the 70's and 80's you could take a real camera into any show. When I photographed the Clash I was a fan first, a photographer second...in the beginning I bought tickets to see the shows and brought my camera along...it was the D.I.Y. ethic the Clash espoused!'

For the 1979 Palladium NYC show I only had one 36 frame roll of colour film and one roll B&W – I was 22 years-old and broke.

My friend Dorothy and I had pretty good orchestra seats and that's where I shot the live shots that can be seen in the opening credits of Danny Garcia's film. When the show was over we went round to the Stage door to wait for the band to come out. From the first face I saw, I started shooting, that was Topper, then Lee Dorsey, and then DJ Barry 'Scratchy' Myers. As Mick Jones came out he headed towards the bus parked at the end of the street. While he walked he talked to fans & signed autographs. I walked backwards taking photo after photo of Mick, Dorothy at my back making sure I didn't trip or run into anyone. I fed off the energy and excitement of the fans and how Mick connected with them. Joe and Paul were just hanging out talking to people, and I got some shots of them. Joe always took time to talk and hang out with fans.

Later, I got guest-listed to see the band at Bond's and there is one shot of Topper fist pumping as he's climbing down off the drum riser which he says is one of his favourite photos of himself. That just amazes me!

Backstage at Bonds I wasn't officially 'press' but Kosmo was nice enough to let me bring my camera. I was in heaven, but also knew this might be a once in a lifetime opportunity. I tried to take fly on the wall shots the whole night, but I did ask Paul & Pearl to pose for me ... one resulting photo of Paul became my first ever published photo, as a full back cover in the British magazine *Teenage Kicks*. I always imagined the photo ripped off and tacked to the walls of Clash fans all over Europe.

One of the best photos of the night was of Joe Strummer. The band was on the other side of a curtain for press photos and I couldn't get in. Dorothy saw I wasn't having the best of luck trying to muscle my way into that little nook where Joe, Mick and Paul were being photographed by the press. She stood on one side of the curtain divider and called me over. 'Streno! Come here! I'll pull the curtain back and you be ready to take the picture'. And so it happened. Dorothy pulled back the curtain. One of us called to Joe. He turned, looked straight into the lens, I focused, framed, and pop, the photo was taken. As soon as it was done, I thanked him, and Joe pulled back the curtain and went about his business on the other side.

Asbury Park 1982 © Joe Streno

'Basically we were fed up with each other,'

Mick Jones

Mad-O-Rama arcade - Joe plays after-party pinball, NYC

Bond's 1981 © Joe Streno

'I think we did something good…probably a mixture of luck and
fortunate timing'   *Mick Jones*

Both pictures on this page Asbury Park 1982 © Joe Streno

'I can't remember the rest of them ever driving a car. Thank goodness, can you imagine Mick Jones at the wheel?'

Jock Scot

Portrait of Paul Simonon and Pearl Harbor 1981 © Joe Streno

'Paul saw himself as a bit of a mediator you know,'

Pete Howard

'Joe wanted to be famous and not famous at the same time,'

Tymon Dogg

Both photos on this page from the 'Secret photo session' 1983 © Mike Laye

'We had to change the team because the atmosphere was too terrible'

Joe Strummer

1983 © Mike Laye

'Elvis has left the building...'

Mick Jones

'I'm guessing that I got the job because I could play and I had the right credentials'

Nick Sheppard

1983 © Mike Laye

'Hundreds of people out there would give their right arm to play in The Clash'.

Joe Strummer

The Rise and Fall of

The Clash

The original documentary script

By Danny Garcia

1981

TV Presenter: ... fans of British Rock group The Clash, but tickets to their long stint in Manhattan were oversold by Bond's Casino

Joe Strummer: Everywhere, everything is no good and everybody's walking around going: this is no good, this won't do, everything's gone wrong - so there's no time to stand around with some nice pair of velvet trousers on, going on about what you gonna do to your woman tonight...

TV reporter: The Clash sold 3500 tickets each for a week of shows...

Paul Simonon: Well, it's like we generally feel like a tie with people that are generally the underdogs, like people that are fighting against the establishment

Interviewer: Do you think it can hurt you supporting political causes?

Paul Simonon: Not if you feel strongly enough about it

TV Presenter: ...the fire Marshall say last night Bond's was crowded beyond legal capacity so if you wanna see The Clash tonight...

Joe Strummer: This ain't no insulting station you know? We don't squat on top of you and drop stuff on your face. We treat people like human beings

Paul Simonon: We don't blow smoke in people's faces so to speak

Mick Jones: People shouldn't expect too much I think and then they'll be pleasantly surprised

Interviewer: Don't expect too much? ...

Mick Jones: Yeah, I think it's very important, right? Instead of demanding from other people to be entertained, perhaps they should learn to do it themselves

TV reporter: What is this band that has created such a fuss?

Chris Salewicz: People say to me: what happened to The Clash? Why did they break up and I always say: well, they went mad and people think I'm joking. I'm not!

Joe Strummer: we have to talk to a lot of journalists and they always ask us: excuse me Sir, but does your music have a message? And if you say yeah then you led yourself in for: oh yeah? Well what is the message? So! For all of those trainee journalists in the audience: this is the message!

Pearl Harbor: When I was hanging around The Clash for so long I definitely felt like I was going to Rock'n'Roll High School...

Tymon Dogg: Mick had his songs, right? And then he got Paul… you know Paul had to work all the time to get on with that bass to even get anywhere and he was there with his look and all the rest of it and then they saw Joe in the 101'ers and Bernie, you know, got him involved. But there were very different roads that were going on there ...

Pearl Harbor: I wanted to figure out what it was that made them so special so I just observed and from what I learned, the band has to have a few things and they had everything.

Terry Chimes: I think the focus and the energy and the intensity was the thing with The Clash. They were very ambitious and very keen to make it happen.

Pearl Harbor: First you have to have a great drummer, if you don't have a great drummer you haven't got a great band. Topper was the best drummer in the whole World according to me...

Kris Needs: Just electrifying, exciting, absolutely manic...

Pearl Harbor: Bass player, Paul. When he first started he couldn't play bass but Paul practiced bass every single day. He had a great style that influenced The Clash and their way of dressing, and he was responsible for always making sure that the visuals were good.

Mike Laye: They had attitude, they had politics, just everything you want in a Rock'n'Roll band, they were tremendous.

Pearl Harbor: Then you have Mick Jones, who is basically a Rock'n'Roll fan, really like, like the Stones, his hero is Keith Richards, Mott The Hopple...

Jock Scot: They were an attractive sort of Beatles like gadabout thing, you know?

Pearl Harbor: So there was Topper the Jazzbo, Paul mostly liked Black music, then Mick's Rock'n'Roll influence with not only the way he looked but the way he thought...

Rudy Fernandez: At that time they were the only band that mattered, best Rock'n'Roll band in the World...

Pearl Harbor: And then there's Joe. Joe was basically a Rhythm & Blues, Blues person, American roots.

Chris Salewicz: The Clash are basically number three. It's the Beatles, The Rolling Stones and The Clash.

Pearl Harbor: So there's four different people who liked four different styles of music and they're all really intelligent and they're all really passionate. And so if you have all those things, you have a great band, you know? And so they worked hard and they were very passionate. Passion is a corny word but that's exactly what The Clash were, they were a really passionate band. And they were the best live band ever...

Pat Gilbert: The Clash are kind of unique amongst all rock bands. They kinda had a higher purpose and I can't think of one other band that you can say that about.

Viv Albertine: I think what's made The Clash really endure it's got to be down to the songwriting and I put that mostly down to Mick or the conflict between Mick and Joe, this artistic conflict between those two which have made so many great, great songs, great choruses... But I also think that the kind of D.I.Y. sense of their clothes and they looked like boys off the street, they talked about ordinary things that everyone was going through and they were angry and there was nothing going on for youth at that time and I think The Clash really sort of embodied that sort of frustration and that anger that we had nothing to do...

Mike Laye: Rock'n'Roll meant an enormous amount to young people in those days. It was the process by which attitudes changed and The Clash were the next wave of revolutionaries...

David Mingay: In the political framework I saw them as political terrorists getting away with murder...

Chris Salewicz: The thing about The Clash really is that it operates on a multiplicity of levels you know, it's like on one hand it's performance art, it's street theatre, it's the poetry of satire really. This whole thing about The Clash being a political group, I never saw them as a political group. I thought they were a satirical group, they were pointing fingers at the things that needed to have fingers pointed at. And they were funny too...

Mick Jones: I think we did something good and that just turned out... probably a mixture of luck and fortunate timing. Timing was very important, but nothing you could have contrived in any way. It just turned out that way.

MEET BERNARD RHODES

Chris Salewicz: Bernie would always describe The Clash early on as 'a very creative situation' and I think he genuinely did believe in that. I think he believed in the group very, very much. And the thing about Bernie as opposed to Malcolm McLaren, his former work partner - I always found Malcolm McLaren to be something of a cold fish really... Bernie actually has a warmth about him, and a humanity, and you can engage with him.

David Mingay: Bernie was I called it an intellectual of fashion and the zeitgeist. When I went to his house in Camden, he had an empty room and in the room were these piles of magazines, *Marxism Today* mainly, and they were piled up high, so about two foot high and he used those instead of chairs. So he was a kind of pseudo-revolutionary and he also studied the intellectual side of Punk and music.

Kris Needs: He - early on got into revolutionary kind of philosophy, he was at the Paris riots - He was like, compared to Malcolm McLaren, Bernie was the real deal...

Mark Helfond: A lot of people didn't know what they wanted to do, or where to go with it but people like Malcolm and Bernard did and I wouldn't say they had a master plan but they forced people in certain directions to question themselves and come up with the right answers and, as you probably gather, they did.

Pete Howard: Bernie would have you believe that him and Malcolm McLaren stood with a row of musicians up against the wall and said right: 'you're in Siouxie & The Banshees, you're in The Clash, you're in the Sex Pistols' and then 'go and try to play your instruments'. And that it was him and Malcolm McLaren that did it, that there were no other influences, that it was them. But I think, I don't know how much Bernie will be remembered as that.

Kris Needs: He was the one who was kind of fuelling McLaren who was a bit of a dilettante and would flee on to the next thing, but a lot of that was Bernie. Bernie came up with the name the Sex Pistols, for a few months, he had to sort of sit there while McLaren took the Pistols to become the most notorious band in the country.

Pete Howard: I think Bernie had the asshole a little bit about the fact that everybody would actually say Malcolm McLaren started Punk and he would be like: 'look, look you know it was me and Malcolm and blah, blah, blah'...

Mike Laye: He had this big competitive thing with Malcolm, 'cause he'd worked with Malcolm in the shop and it was sort of Malcolm had gone off and got a band and it felt like now Bernie had gone off and got a band.

Viv Albertine: Bernie Rhodes to me is like the Emperor's new clothes. He's just someone who's pumped himself up into something that he wasn't really as a person, as a man, as a manager, he was very much always on the coat tails of Malcolm McLaren, trying to copy his way but without the finesse, without the charm and without the artistic vision. He was just always like this little guy following other people, he came muscling in with The Clash, I don't know why they took so much notice of him, I suppose he did work hard for them.

Kris Needs: He wanted a band that would almost be his mouthpiece. He had an agenda that he wanted this band to fill. He knew Mick, when they had The London SS with Tony James and that was kind of ... Mick still had really long hair and they were doing MC5 songs. The Clash, everything had to be Year Zero and different and new and Bernie kind of, he really did have that band work.

Tymon Dogg: I think he was good for what they were doing, definitely. He was good, he got them off the ground... don't think it would have happened without him.

Pearl Harbor: A lot of people say: if you have a good manager, you're 50% ahead of the game and Joe and Paul specially loved Bernie and he did bring so much great stuff to the table that I can't make fun of it, he wound them up in the right way, he told them not to be pussies, he said you know, 'Don't talk about love and don't talk about cars, talk about politics'.

Vic Godard: Bernard Rhodes is like really you got to consider him as a member of The Clash because he did put obviously a lot of ideas into the band. So it's a very unusual situation where you get like a manager who is not aloof from the band, is actually part of the creative process of it I suppose.

Terry Chimes: I would say he's not a good manager and he didn't understand how to keep things together, how to solve problems. He only understood this sort of conflict management...having said that, you wouldn't have The Clash if Bernie hadn't done that.

Mick Jones: He's a very intelligent guy, he's always thinking outside the box and always got something to say in terms of what you should do, which is very good if you need to know what you need to do, but when you... You should always remain open to things and Bernie was very challenging and that kind of gets your mind going, you know so it's a big part of things. The only trouble is that he wasn't sharing with us as much as he should have done probably.

Vic Godard: Because he didn't like telling you what he was organizing, he liked to sort of surprise you with things, you know?

Kris Needs: You can't take away Bernie's ideas. I mean, you used to hear conflicting opinions of Bernie apart from the - he was an easy figure of fun for the band to, you know plant a piece of cheese on his head while you're talking to him so you can collapse laughing when he's telling you about the Paris riots...

Mike Laye: Bernie had much more influence on the band than a normal manager, he didn't just deal with the contracts and the organization of the tours and stuff... the record company... he was really active in the organization of the band. Kinda like you hear the stories of Brian Epstein with The Beatles, or The Who, Rolling Stones managers, almost a sort of an extra member of the band and Bernie was very much that.

Pearl Harbor: He was always bullying them and egging them on to wind them up because he would get a reaction, and a reaction in Punk Rock music is what it's all about so in that respect he was brilliant but as a human being who you want to sit next to on the bus, no.

Viv Albertine: Bernie Rhodes would arrive at the door, I'd open the door, he'd push pass me up the stairs and not speak a word to me, not even look me in the eye. He's a rude, socially inept person.

Ray Jordan: Asshole... sorry he's an asshole.

Pearl Harbor: Bernie and I didn't speak, we didn't like each other, he's totally a misogynistic person so he never confided in me, in my opinion, for anything. If he came to our house I would open the door and he would stomp right pass me and not even say hello...

Nick Sheppard: Bernie's managerial style? ...mmm, don't get me started. Bernie's interpersonal relationships are complicated to say the least and he's not really a people person.

Ray Jordan: Managerial style? Talks a lot of crap but at least he gets you working, you always work with Bernie Rhodes. He always gets you on the road and you have more work, he puts you through work, work, work, work, work but he doesn't know how to treat people.

Jock Scot: Bernie's managerial technique as such, if that existed, was something which was obscure but I know that Joe leaned heavily on his opinion. You know, like: what do we do next? What are we doing? What does it all mean? Bernie could always reduce it to a sort of simple political thing. Bernie was really a revolutionary, he saw it in political terms not in financial showbiz terms.

Kris Needs: One thing that we must bear in mind is that Bernie was a second hand car salesman when he started as the band's manager. He had that mentality, he might have been politically correct but he was from an old school of managers where you did take your percentage...

Jock Scot: But I thought it got a bit Stalinist at times, you know? Not necessarily just from Bernie but those music papers of the time, you know: Sounds, Melody Maker, NME. They were all like: what are The Clash doing? They got 50 quid a week each? How can they sing about the poor oppressed people?

Kris Needs: Bernie was a Mod as well, he was very well versed in Tin Pan Alley biz maneuvers, the Mod scene and all that so he knew a lot, his knowledge was great and he tried to implement all this but what he didn't bank on was The Clash's own personalities emerging which happened through '77.

Pat Gilbert: I think Bernie is one of the unsung heroes of music management. I just think it was great that he brought this kind of mad anarchic political energy to the band and that he ran the band like it was some kind of military operation where people were expendable and feelings came kind of second to the main mission. And you know, he had ideas and he didn't wanna to be conventional, he wanted to be unorthodox in order to shake things up and make the band a cultural event and if The Clash were anything they were this big cultural event, that's why we're talking about them now.

Kris Needs: I mean he was great for ideas and he, you know the visual side of things, he liked winding up record companies, he had a lot of really good points. I mean there was never a dull moment. You certainly could not call him a boring manager and you would talk to him and sometimes I felt sorry for him 'cause he's sitting there, poor bloke is on fire... you know what I mean? Or he's covered in lettuce while he's talking to Lester Bangs, who thought this must be the... Lester Bangs sort of went: 'do all groups do this to their managers?' (Laughs)

DON'T ARGUE... BERNIE'S BACK

Pearl Harbor: Before Bernie came back they had Blackhill Management and they were all great people as well, it was a whole organization... but I think they just, The Clash felt they were just too nice and safe for them, nobody was winding them up except for Kosmo and they actually did kind of need that at the time for inspiration.

David Mingay: Blackhill came in who had been the Pink Floyd managers and they put in a much more professional angle. They'd stayed in slightly better hotels and they went on tour with the group... but I think that they did rely on Bernie's creativity and that came back when Joe wanted to go back with Bernie... and I remember I once said to him: well, Bernie knows about, really knows about how to put the message, and what kind of messages to (cut)

Kris Needs: Bernie had been sacked then they came back, probably cap in hand, you know? Please come back and save us. He wasn't gonna blow it this time, he was gonna assert himself...

Ray Jordan: Then Bernie Rhodes came along and got 'em away from there and took over.

Mark Helfond: The group, to my way of thinking, had gone down the route of being a Rock'n'Roll band. All the trappings, all the evils of what a Rock'n'Roll band is supposed to do. They lost their way, they lost what made them special. And I understand it was Joe who insisted that Bernard come back and sort it out. To give them fresh impetus, to give them new ideas.

Mick Jones: We were reeling out of control completely, yeah... and he was like, he sensed that. It's not that we wanted to be in control but we were just like drifting in space I reckon.

Rudy Fernandez: You always heard them, when Bernie wasn't there, they were always talking about him! It's like they missed him, you know?

Pearl Harbor: They weren't comfortable with things running around smoothly and so whenever Bernie was around things like became chaos and madness and that's what they liked. They didn't want somebody backstage saying: 'that was a great show', even though that's what I was always thinking and saying, you know? But they wanted somebody to wind em up after the show and say: 'ahh what was that bollocks?' or whatever, you know? That's what they liked at the time. Joe and Paul that is, I think Mick was a bit more happy being comfortable. So it was mostly Joe and Paul that wanted Bernie.

Rudy Fernandez: He brought like a lot of nervous creative tension, you know? There was always a lot of yelling and stuff going on, you know?

Mick Jones: Then Bernie coming back and then he kind of like - what he did was - he wanted to sack everybody, all our crew and stuff so there was like - and everybody seemed to be going along with it and I wouldn't, I didn't want to go along with it. All the guys that had been working with us for so long and they wanted to sack them!

Kris Needs: Mick hated the fact Bernie was back -

Ray Jordan: Because he always thought he was out to scam him.

Mick Jones: I'm watching you!

Ray Jordan: He always knew that there was something to do with his money or something like that, he was out to scam him. But he had him sussed from the beginning but to keep Joe sweet he went along with it.

Chris Townsend: Bernie I suppose was a strong influence over Joe and maybe a sort of fatherly figure. I suppose he also gave him a lot of confidence. Bernie was probably talking the right politics, he was probably the person that inspired Joe's kind of, I would say socialist attitude, in a sense.

Kris Needs: Joe was the one who wanted the edge put back in the band and he felt with Bernie you had that edge, whereas the rest of the band didn't have that much respect – I mean Paul did a big mural that was on the wall of Rehearsals of a naked Bernie getting shat on by pigeons – it's all this... it was quite cruel really and didn't show any respect whatsoever but Joe felt he gave the band an edge.

Pearl Harbor: Bernie did inspire them when he got back together with the band, like I said he was always winding them up, which is what they wanted. In some ways to be a ruthless manager it's really great because Bernie is not liked by anybody but that suits The Clash's purposes fine, they didn't need anybody to like Bernie. They wanted him to be a hard-ass, they wanted him to go on the record company and demand things, which he did and he accomplished.

MR. KOSMO VINYL

Jock Scot: I lived with Kosmo Vinyl who became The Clash's publicist. He was obsessed by The Clash before he worked for them...

Reporter: What do you do for The Clash?

Kosmo Vinyl: Whatever needs doing anything, wash a pair of socks, go see the record company...

Kris Needs: He became their mouthpiece and assumed a position which didn't do a lot for the original Clash ethos because like Johnny Green felt that his place had been taken and Johnny was much a part of the band during you know the '77-'78 period, he was essential to - without Johnny the band might not have even made it to rehearsal some days, he was vital to the group, and when Kosmo came along he called him 'a usurper'. That was the name he liked to use. You know Johnny felt he didn't have a function anymore and the band were going, heading off in another way that he wasn't interested in so basically they swapped Johnny for Kosmo.

Pearl Harbor: When Johnny Green left, everybody was sad including myself because he was such a great character. I think he left for the right reasons, I think he was such a smart, brilliant guy because he loved it when they were broke and they were all winding each other up and causing trouble and doing runners and, you know, misbehaving, but once The Clash started becoming successful it wasn't nearly as much fun for him and he sort of felt that he had done what he needed to do, plus, you know, he had a lot of substance abuse problems and things were getting the better of him -

Rudy Fernandez: Kosmo was like the fifth member of The Clash, you know? He was always there, you know...he lived and breathed The Clash, you know?

Ray Jordan: Kosmo was the press man, he used to work with Ian Dury before as a press man and Kosmo could get anything done.

Kris Needs: He liked to think he looked like Elvis when he was young, kind of with - you know he had all the clothes, the quiff and he influenced the way the band looked with that kind of - this is the stuff you stick on your hair... He steamed in basically.

Terry Chimes: There's no name for what Kosmo did because he was a spokesperson, he was handling the press, but he was with us all the time and he was entertaining everyone, he was like the life and soul of the party. Telling jokes and you know? Bringing everyone together...

Nick Sheppard: He was a very important part of the whole set up and he kept the kind of spirit of the thing, not being a musician, not being in the band, he was like the kind of... he was kind of the keeper of the flame I guess you'd say.

Pete Howard: I suppose he was like a spin doctor really, he was kinda the person who gave - he would take the ordinary and try to make it fly - you know. He was very personable, very social, knew lots of people, a lot of people liked him. He knew where the parties were, where the clothes were, what was cool, what wasn't cool.

Pearl Harbor: He knew all the right people to speak with in the Rock'n'Roll World in the UK because he'd been dealing with them and he was bright enough to know who he thought would be the right people to speak with The Clash so your publicity agent is more than important and Kosmo was the most brilliant PR person anyone could ever wish for.

Terry Chimes: Joe and Kosmo are quite similar 'cause they both hated success, both hated the trappings of success. Fancy cars or whatever, they hated that. And they loved that kind of idea of being in a conflict the whole time...Kosmo, again enjoyed chaos, enjoyed - never liked being comfortable so he fitted really well in that way.

Kris Needs: Again, another bloke Joe could relate to 'cause he was diametrically opposed to Mick's Hip-Hop thing. I mean, I don't think Kosmo really got that one, but when it came to doing a quiff and an Elvis then - you know; he was another guy that Joe liked...

CLASH IN TIMES SQUARE NYC

Kosmo Vinyl: Everybody who's got a Bond's ticket has got to wait a few days but everybody will get in or get their money back, that we promise...

Radio Reporter: Over-crowding and court battles are killing the Clash concerts, that's how it seems. There was a lot of shouting and screaming on Broadway in front of Bond's Disco when it was announced that the matinee of The Clash was cancelled, police on horses were used to break up the crowd, needless to say the fans were really infuriated about that...

Joe Strummer: We just went to New York to play seven dates in a club there - but when we got there, the whole thing blew up and we made it on to the like News at 10 and TV and the national channel networks, something that we hadn't done before... it turned out that because the police shut the club down and then the fire department and then the building department there was a lot of people jamming up Times Square complaining about their tickets and how they came in from Nantucket Island and they didn't have enough bus fare to go back, come back the next week so we ended up doing 17 shows there 'cause we could only play to half buildings at the time according to the new rules!

Kris Needs: The Bond's residency was possibly one of the greatest things that The Clash did. It was so important in breaking them - for The Clash to bring New York to a standstill and get on the evening news and to invite - and this was Bernie's instigation - Grand Master Flash and New York Post-Punk groups like ESG on the bill, The Treacherous Three...

Pearl Harbor: From the moment the kids arrived at Bond's they'd be listening to old records it would be all bands that The Clash liked including Kurtis Blow, who the audience hated and stuff like that so...

Radio Reporter: The Clash were to do 8 shows at Bond's but when the disco packed in more than 3600 fans - the club only legally holds 1800 - all the trouble began.

Pearl Harbor: That was really exciting, 'specially for me too because it was three weeks at Bond's, it was like Beatle-mania in terms of fans screaming, none of that shit had ever happened, police everywhere and each show was sold out to capacity and I was the DJ!

Kris Needs: It was the cross pollination of New York at that time which was a magic period in itself and somehow Bernie managed to place The Clash from West London smack in the middle of Manhattan and make them the centre-point of the whole New York explosion going on at that time.

Pat Gilbert: Mick was very passionate about Dance music at that time, they spent a lot of time in New York and he was into Hip-Hop. And Hip-Hop and Rap was all about kind of Dance remixes, spending time in the studio elongating stuff, you know...

percussion, all the kind of bells and whistles that had nothing to do really with the more straight forward Rock'n'Roll template that I think Joe and Paul kind of preferred...

Kris Needs: When they were going to NY and Mick got into Hip Hop, I think that's when they started really going in different directions...

Chris Salewicz: One of the things about Joe, having been a Pub rocker, was that he always knew when to return to a Chuck Berry song or a Chuck Berry feel anyway. And he was kinda, you know he was quite conservative with his musical taste, Joe - Joe wants to kind of do the sort of really probably straight Rock'n'Roll songs and Mick's more much interested in Hip-Hop in the kind of emerging Rap culture, new music generally you know?

Mick Jones: I used to get on their nerves because of it a bit, because I was so enthusiastic about it - it was just a kind of different thing then, but he didn't really liked it much at the time. I think I must have got on their nerves 'cause I was so enthusiastic about it but...

Kris Needs: I think that's when they started really going into different directions. Joe kicked back to Rockabilly, Mick meanwhile had got into New York radio and the whole Hip-Hop culture which was only just emerging then. They were one of the first bands to mix the two: Hip-Hop and Rock'n'Roll and they'd already done it with Reggae.

RAT PATROL VS *COMBAT ROCK*

Chris Salewicz: One of the things about *Combat Rock* is that it's the first album that's been made since Bernie Rhodes has returned so he wants a commercial record and he's very certain of this. And Mick's already been reined in by his instructions and he's telling Mick to write commercial songs. But Mick does insist that the record is made in New York, which the others didn't want because it runs up the bills a lot, among other things.

Jock Scot: There was some big argument about recording in New York, which I recall as being a big deal at the time, this New York thing.

Pearl Harbor: In London the pubs close at 11 o'clock, there isn't much really to do at night except for wander around and go to people's houses and maybe find some after-hours club which is usually full of creepy people, but New York is open 24 hours a day including food, booze, craziness, anything you want is in New York and they really enjoyed that, it was an inspiration for them.

Joe Strummer: We started to get attached to Electric Ladyland around that time so we booked that again and went in and it was quite quick really.

Kris Needs: Mick started experimenting again when he'd done his final album which was *Rat Patrol From Fort Bragg* which was based on a sixties wartime TV series called Rat Patrol...

Chris Salewicz: There's a lot of material and some of it it's quite experimental like *Kill Time*, and *The Beautiful People Are Ugly Too* which I think is fantastic, sounds like a Kinks B-side...

Tymon Dogg: Bernie... I remember him coming in and making a criticism that there were too many things going on, that there wasn't one direction 'cause he wanted to really get back to a bit like the first album where you put it on and you find every track is more or less the same. It doesn't suddenly go off...

Joe Strummer: But we had a problem with the mix of it...

Kris Needs: Mick started experimenting again...

Chris Salewicz: And then they go on the tour of Japan and Australia, Hong Kong, Thailand. And in Australia they have this crazy idea they're gonna mix it after they've done the shows when all their ears are shot, a complete waste of time...

Joe Strummer: We had some gigs in Australia so we tried taking it down there and mixing it after the shows but that's a very tough thing...

Chris Salewicz: - and presumably adds to their general exhaustion and I think part of the problem is obviously that - as happens to a lot of groups - they're all completely exhausted, they're all completely done in, so no one is thinking sensibly, really.

Joe Strummer: We ended up with a lot of music, a lot of tapes and I wanted to boil it down unto one album and stop mucking around and refine it down to the essence. And Mick was into 'let's have a 12" or two 12" with the album' and I wouldn't have minded, if the tracks had merited it, but I felt that they were all too long, it was becoming too self-indulgent. And I felt like the opposite.

Mick Jones: That was the time when we found out we couldn't... I didn't know how to mix records anymore.

Pat Gilbert: There were several kind of key events towards the end of the band, which kind of went against Mick. I mean there were decisions that were made against Mick, the mixing of *Combat Rock* was definitely one of those...

Joe Strummer: We had to call Glyn Johns in at the last minute to mix the album. Because we had made an attempt to mix it ourselves that we hadn't been able to do. Glyn Johns mixed it in a week...

Kris Needs: And in the end they gave it to Glynn Johns, who'd worked with the Stones and Elton John and he basically ruthlessly pruned it and because Mick was so hurt at getting his version rejected he didn't contribute to Glynn John's remixing and editing, he was like: 'no!' You know and – so Joe did it with Glynn Johns and *Combat*

Rock came out as a punchier album but still with a lot of elements of Mick's more experimental leanings.

Chris Salewicz: Bernie gets Glyn Johns to remix the album. Joe is there very early, Mick - as is his tradition - arrives rather late by which time half his stuff the first day, some of his stuff's been taken off already, you know?

TV Host: Mick Jones of The Clash!

Joe Strummer: He saved the album really and Mick, his view was that I ruined his music and stuff like this...

Chris Salewicz: He didn't like it... but now actually he does think it was the right way to mix it...

Mick Jones: I think it was a good job that it came out as one, *Combat Rock*. It was good after all that, it was a bit painful at the time but it's a much better record than the other one, so that was another one of those cymbal level things. It was probably the best thing to do at the time. We were all floundering a bit by that time and it was good he kind of whipped it into shape you know and time showed it was the best thing to do. Like I said before no one remembers how loud the cymbals were after a few years you know what I mean? Why get upset about it?

Pat Gilbert: I think it's quite wounding if you spend a lot of time kind of creating an album or mixing an album an then someone comes along and says: look, we don't like it, we're gonna change it, we're gonna get an outside agent - who in this case was the producer Glyn Johns - to tidy this all up and make it - well not a completely different record but a kind of a shorter, sharper more focused record, I think, when Mick was trying to make it the opposite of that. You know, that can't be anything but hurtful to somebody. But then that was The Clash! The Clash... one of the good things about The Clash is that... you know there wasn't a great amount of sentimentality between the members in the way they conducted themselves most of the time and it's good, it goes back to that kind of boot camp army military thing, that the higher purpose it's more important than people's feelings.

JOE GOES A.W.O.L

Kosmo (*audio tape*): Joe, if you're listening, please get in touch... we need to talk to you!

Kris Needs: That was something that went a bit wrong for Bernie. Originally they were gonna start touring, and it's commonly assumed that tickets weren't going very well and that they'd had to pull some publicity stunt to sell more tickets - i.e. make Joe disappear. But it wasn't quite like that… Joe really decided that he really did want to have a bit of a break; Bernie decided to make it look like he'd disappeared and then - all Joe done he'd bummed off somewhere...

Jock Scot: The Clash were playing in Scotland, the first date of that tour which never was, was in Dundee. So I travelled up to Dundee and they said, 'The concert's been cancelled, Joe Strummer has gone missing'. and I'm like... 'fuck Joe! I've hitch-hiked up from Edinburgh! And I don't know anybody in Dundee! I'm gonna have to go back there now!'...

Joe Strummer: Yeah I just dropped out of a UK tour and I went to Paris instead and got drunk.

Kris Needs: He did end up in Paris, doing the marathon. He went a lot longer than anyone thought and Bernie, particularly - who sort of encouraged this little disappearing act to shake up the band and get some publicity - was, I think, rather surprised 'cause Joe grew a beard and he had to be tracked down at this address in Paris and brought back.

Jock Scot: I think it was stupid but it does show you that at the time - this is after *London Calling* is released - they couldn't sell out small venues in the UK! That's why Bernie said: 'fuck off, we haven't sold all the tickets!' It shows you how the myth has taken over now - The Clash, The Clash, The Clash! At the time they weren't selling out average venues in the UK!

TOPPER & THE DRUG ISSUE

Viv Albertine: Mick was really clean at the beginning when I was with him, he didn't even smoke spliffs, all he did was drink sort of lukewarm tea... and Joe, I know, came from the sort of squat scene in West London, which was very spliffy, lots of grass and hash and that kind of thing so I think he brought that with him.

Pearl Harbor: When I first met them, like, Joe and Mick might have liked coke a little bit but what happened, I think, in the late seventies, they had all agreed that in order to be a good, functioning for the people - you know - Punk band, you can't be taking drugs like coke, a rich's persons drug, which also makes people talk bullshit, you know stuff like coke, so they had all agreed that they were drinkers and smokers so that was gonna be what The Clash were. They smoked dope and drank. And everybody liked to drink a lot. But what happened was Topper started sneaking off doing this and that, I don't know if Mick was sneaking off doing this and that but I know that Joe and Paul just stuck to the smoking dope and drinking and that made everything - you know OK - in terms that they were all on the same page.

Rudy Fernandez: They loved to smoke, you know, a little pot, California pot, you know? So they go, 'Where can we get some?' So I go and I call my friend Glenn, Glenn is a big pot dealer in San Francisco and I go: 'Glenn you gotta get down, come down to Monterey you know… we're with these guys, we're gonna have a great time you know? Bring some stuff!' And he goes, 'Well, how much do you want me to bring?' I said, 'Bring it all!' You know? So in a couple of hours he's down there with like a duffel bag full of stuff...

Ray Jordan: In Japan, you can't get a spliff in Japan. I remember getting a little tiny spliff of hash and the guy said he wanted to share it with him 'cause of who he was and he just took it, left the guy standing outside, went into the toilet, had it and told the guy, 'Thank you very much!' You know, he couldn't work without having - getting up in the morning and having his first spliff so anytime you hear he says he's not going until spliff comes... that is quite true. In Japan you just get loads of alcohol and somehow they would get crushed aspirins and things like that - oh yeah! To keep, yeah - different things - Crushed aspirins and everything just to keep them going, you know?

Pat Gilbert: Well I think The Clash it wasn't a church picnic, they were a Rock'n'Roll band, they were young guys, young cool guys living in the world of Rock'n'Roll and it's about when any aspect of anyone's lifestyle becomes a problem that's when the problem is...

Pearl Harbor: I remember like in the recording studio things like: hey, where's Topper? And then you would know that he was in the bathroom doing drugs and everybody would roll their eyes, including me, because he was the drummer on my album at the time...So you loved him so much and you knew that he was such a great musician, he didn't fuck up on the drums so you can't really yell at someone unless they're fucking up so everyone just tried to be patient with Topper and hope that he was gonna stop, you know, being like that. But he got further and further and further into drugs and not caring about the purpose of the band or anything like that...

Tymon Dogg: Yeah, he'd borrow any note of you for approximately three minutes and then hand you it back rolled up, yeah. 'Is that alright?' Well, yes of course.

Topper: Yeah I'll manage, you know. Give me some more of that.

Jock Scot: Topper was marginalized from the very beginning really, he was the drummer from Dover. You know, he wasn't a London boy and all the press focus was on the other three, never on Topper, and he was a big part of the band, his fucking drumming held it together, you know? So Topper started to spend more time on the road with the crew and some of the crew were heavy drug takers and that's where his drug habit really mushroomed.

Pearl Harbor: One of my last memories before they let him go was - he knocked on our door and I opened up, early in the morning and I opened up the door and there is Topper with chocolate all over his face and all over his clothes and I thought he had been all beat up so I was shocked, I said, 'Topper what happened?' And he was like, 'What? What? Everything's alright!' And I said, 'What's that all over you?' And he was like, 'What? What?' And he looks down and he sees that he has chocolate all over, 'Oh me and Donna had a chocolate fight in bed', so I was like, I just said, 'Ok, well come on in' and Paul saw him and it was just so obvious - here is Topper walking around London and taking the tube with - I'm not exaggerating, he had chocolate all over himself. So that was kinda like a big indication, I know it sounds petty but it was a real indication of how fucked up the guy was - and it was sad and everything, but it was, it's eyeball rolling, oh God, what the fuck are you supposed to do with that?

Kris Needs: In terms of new drummers that had come along in that decade, Topper was the best. Topper was the engine room as Joe liked to call him.

Chris Townsend: Topper was a genius at what he done and I completely applaud his energy. He was a great performer and every show he would come off that stage completely exhausted and maybe, you know, that was the weak point for him.

Pearl Harbor: Even though he was always a great drummer, his behavior just became a little too much to handle and when you realize that he wasn't contributing to the grooviness of the band, you know? He didn't stand for what they stood for, they lost patience with him. I wish they hadn't 'cause they knew that Topper was the best drummer in the whole World too but they just couldn't tolerate the junkiness stuff so that's what happened.

Ray Jordan: Topper was the only one who was heavily into that sort of thing and it took me a long time to find out. I found out properly in New Zealand when he started shaking and I didn't know what was wrong with him and everybody realized - they seemed to know who was on it and they'll find it. So one minute he's down and then you'll know he's got something. Or you'll find in the hotel funny people turn up any time at night, spend the whole night up, and you'll find anybody who takes heroin lies to you, always lie to you and you never know how to take 'em or if to trust them and that's when I knew really, because many times he let me down.

Jock Scot: When Topper became a full blown addict, which he was, then really they've should have said, 'Topper is ill, let's get him some treatment, some help and we'll step back for six months or however long it takes'! But instead, he was sacked, that's not very good is it?

Pearl Harbor: Well it was pretty soon after the chocolate incident. They, The Clash came over to where we were living and - I kinda couldn't handle it so I made myself scarce and they went outside and I know Topper got really upset and I don't like to think about that kinda stuff.

Mick Jones: I thought we could work something out, but the times were like, you needed it now, and we didn't have it then so that's what happens. But I didn't want that to happen, not at all, but that did happen and that was probably inevitable as well. You can't run a thing if you're - so yeah you're a drug band, sure, but that just gets too much after a while either way.

Pearl Harbor: Joe and Paul and Mick were really sad about it but they felt they had no choice. And I think Topper was really shocked and hurt and was hoping that hey, give me another chance, but they didn't feel like giving him another chance.

Jock Scot: And I don't think that reflects badly on the band - more on the attitude at the time, you know people were, he's a drug addict and that was it. End of story. You just put a big cross through someone who was a heroin addict, you knew they were useless and that they would lie to you and steal and be unreliable. But I think his drug addiction affected his timing as a drummer as it would, you know, if you're on a sort of downer then you're not gonna be able to be all over the kit like he used to be.

Pat Gilbert: They didn't wanna take a year off and let someone sort out their problems, they just wanted to steam on and change the World and Topper was a victim of that. But musically it affected the band greatly, they were never ever gonna be as good musically after Topper went as they were before 'cause he was a fabulous musician.

Kris Needs: The start of the end for the Clash was when Topper was sacked, I mean that was unavoidable I suppose but they would admit later that they could have done a lot more to help him rather than just push him out! It took the engine room and it took one of the four members out, it was you know a bit like chucking Ringo out of The Beatles, Charlie Watts out of The Stones. It was kind of that serious for them...

Mickey Gallagher: He couldn't have gone on but it was regrettable that Topper got the habits that he did because other than that he was a great drummer but those habits made him so unreliable and you can't have an unreliable drummer, you know?

Tymon Dogg: I thought he was in fantastic shape as a musician, see like - I mean I think it was just a sort of conservativeness. I don't advocate anybody being hooked on anything - but from my point of view, and later from Joe's point of view - he probably realized that, you know, they were producing the work and I think it was over the top... it was more the fear of a dependent drug getting into the band than what it was actually doing to Topper. It was more of a mental thing, that particularly Joe had, that if heroin came in it would be destructive.

Mick Jones: If you can't do it, you can't do it you get to a point when you can't do it anymore... you're too messed up man.

Ray Jordan: He felt it more than the others because like - they had this connection going and it was like his little brother so he knew he had to go to clean his act 'cause it was getting really bad, really bad, but that's like the state he was carrying himself around. He'd always get on the stage and play! Come the show, I've never known him to slip up on the show itself but the daily business of going around, dirty, and just stayed in his room all day, curtains drawn, nobody sees him... you could tell he's going down so he had to get his act together.

Pat Gilbert: Was it necessary to fire Topper? In the context of The Clash... yeah, I think it was. They didn't have to, I mean it was just this whole thing about the band not being able to have any sort of passengers or any kind of, like, great sentimentality between them, he was deemed to be a problem and they kind of got rid of him. I mean, it's quite sort of harsh but one thing about The Clash is that they never really thought about the consequences of what they were doing. And partly because they didn't want to be a normal kind of Rock'n'Roll band.

THE RETURN OF TERRY CHIMES

Joe Strummer: ... Say hello to Mr. Terry Chimes on drums –

Chris Salewicz: When they brought back Terry Chimes back into the crew I thought it was a touch of genius! I kind of thought, well they would, wouldn't they? Of course they would. There was this sort of poetry about the flow of The Clash and the people around them and it was quite complex actually 'cause there was a synchronicity about the actions of The Clash which suggested that they were a pure intuitive art movement really.

Mick Jones: Terry's great, it was good that Terry came back, you know what I mean? 'cause he was with us originally so it's still part of the same thing. There's a continuity to that that was really good.

Jock Scot: Terry Chimes wasn't the drummer Topper was. Very few people are, certainly not Terry and I think Terry would be the first to admit that Topper Headon was a World Class drummer and that he was a fourth division drummer. But who else could they get? You know? He simplified the drum parts and did the job! He looked the part and it wasn't necessary to audition a hundred ex-hippies, they just got Terry back, sensible - welcome back Terry!

Pearl Harbor: Topper was THE musical genius and Terry Chimes is a great drummer but he's not a genius! God bless him... He's a wonderful guy and a great drummer but he wasn't as great as Topper plus you know when they were songwriting Topper was really important, like I said, adding things so that the songs weren't so samey and so on.

Ray Jordan: You could tell the music changed. The beat wasn't there, you could tell and Topper had a certain way of bashing the drums, you knew it was somebody else. There was no other drummer like him so everybody - you could tell from the crowd's reaction and all -

Mick Jones: I liked to play with Terry as well, yeah, both of them are fantastic drummers you know. I still enjoyed playing the numbers and stuff, there was still most of the time it was still pretty good when we were up on the stage.

Kris Needs: They should have got like a really good session drummer or a guy from another band, like The Who did with Kenny Jones, something like that, just somebody who was a really powerful drummer and they could sort of build on that.

Pat Gilbert: It was a necessity. This is how The Clash worked, right? They had a week to find a new drummer and as far as I understand it they didn't even have any rehearsals, full band rehearsals before they started the American tour 'cause Paul had already left to go to America.

Terry Chimes: They always did do things in a chaotic way, that's part of the conflict and the chaos that they - I think all of us secretly enjoyed all the chaos in a peculiar way, I know that sounds odd but everyone had a dread of routine and comfort and loved chaos so we made chaos - you know? And calling me like a few days really... well it's a few days really because by the time they contacted me and I came down and met and we decided to do it and we had to rush down to rehearse and Paul had to go off to America before for some reason, we had to rehearse without Paul, with Mick playing the bass...

Pat Gilbert: So this is a band playing major stadiums at the top of their game and they do something where the consequence is that they get a drummer in straight off and Terry was a professional enough player to slot in with that and they sounded good, you know? They sounded good. He was a great drummer, I think the problem would have been if they tried to record with him...

Terry Chimes: I was quite shocked how varied it was, I was quite shocked how far they'd gone. And I'd heard the singles 'cause you heard them on the radio but I hadn't heard the albums, I was surprised how much diversity there was in it.

Kris Needs: In some ways it was good getting Terry back but I think it was hopeless no matter who they would have got then, 'cause Topper had gone and it wasn't - it wasn't the same and after Topper had gone, Mick's days were numbered.

COMBAT ROCK ON TOUR 1982

Terry Chimes: It felt to me that the first time round they were arguing with me and now they were arguing with each other, that's the first thing. Bernie's role had changed, he was less in control and he was more getting orders from Joe rather than giving you orders, that was kind of reversed. Big audiences of course and more money around - we were very hand to mouth in the early days, there was no money around - whereas later we could travel more efficiently, eat in restaurants rather than - you know - living like hobos or whatever. So that changed.

Jock Scot: They never had any money when we ran around with them, they were always skint.

Rudy Fernandez: I took them to a Salsa club one night, all of a sudden, you know - these Mexican girls, these Mexican girls go, one of them go, 'Hey! You're those *Combat Rock* guys!' you know? 'Rock The Casbah!' And I was like, I couldn't believe it! You know the home-girls, they even know who they are! I was like, 'Wow! You guys really made it now', you know?

Mick Jones: It was kind of interesting to see how far we'd got and what it was like to play that kind of thing and how strange it was with our numbers and what we were about being in that arena style thing it was a very interesting memorable thing...

Pearl Harbor: The band were really happy because how can you not be, in your twenties and not be really happy that you're succeeding, and that the people are liking it, and that you're getting all this dough? But the dough can be the problem because it's kind of a cliché to say that people write their best music when they're starving. Well, people say that for a good reason and you know when they had all their angst and energy and were rebelling 'cause everything was fucked up with them, they had no money and blah, blah, blah... it was, you know, the fight was for real but when you have money the fight becomes... goes in another direction, that's why they really had to concentrate on politics to keep the fight and the Robin Hood thing going, you know?

Viv Albertine: They were best when they were small and angry and not the stadium rockers, they were still a great stadium Rock band and you know American audiences love that and everything but I think for me and for British audiences they were at their best when they were hard and angry and poor and talking about the injustices of the World kind of thing, well of our little World not the bigger World.

Chris Salewicz: When they cracked it really with *Combat Rock*, everything seemed a bit frenetic and everyone seemed to be a bit generally stressed actually.

Terry Chimes: During that year, '82, we did an awful lot of touring, went everywhere and did lots of work. Probably worked too hard I think and there was a tension developed between Mick on one side and Joe and Paul on the other. And with me just kind of not taking any sides in it, not wanting to take sides really, just wanted to get on with the job I suppose. Because a lot of what they were unhappy about, pre-dated me, was there before I came along, so I thought: this is not my war, I'm not really... you know, a part of this. But that tension built throughout that year and I think because the tension was there, the more they cranked up the heat and made us work harder and harder, the more that tension... it was like a Hot House, you know? Just got hotter and hotter and in the end, you can't carry on like that, something has to blow.

Ray Jordan: Really it was so much work that it was killing Joe. It was just work, work, work.

Chris Salewicz: when you work with that pressure no one's thinking, it's endless, you're touring, when you arrive into town, you're promoting the show, you're promoting the record on the radio, you're doing interviews... there's no time for yourself to sit down and think about what's going on with your life and what's going with what you're doing, with your art, with your creativity. And I think they did, they really kind of imploded through a sort of madness that took over. Maybe everyone was infected with it. But Joe certainly was.

Mark Helfond: I'm led to believe that he was very, very scared that something may happen to him. He got very, very paranoid. Rumors about John Lennon being shot by the FBI, that Mark Chapman was actually primed by the FBI...

Mick Jones: I was under immense pressure, so Bernie said to me, 'Mick, why don't you give your lawyer powers of attorney and then I can work it out with him?'... You know what I mean? I kind of felt under pressure at the time and I said 'OK' for that period and then he went to the other and went, 'Look what Mick's done, he doesn't wanna talk to you anymore he wants you to talk to his lawyer', and then fucked everything up; so that was what happened backstage, you know, but backstage it was always a bit chaotic, it was manipulative.... because we weren't being told what was going on so by that time we've stopped talking to each other a bit - or more than a bit. We've stopped pretty much talking to each other because we were on our own trip so we didn't know what we were doing, we were just like a bunch of idiots thrown into the spotlight, you know?

Kris Needs: it was like an unstoppable monster and it was gonna become - at that point - they were gonna become the biggest band in the World! And I don't think Mick was grumbling about that! I later found out that by this time I think Joe and Paul and Bernie were already plotting the right time for Mick to be sacked...

Pearl Harbor: Well I always heard various discussions about that but I didn't think it would ever happen. I knew they were disgruntled with him, it was - it had a lot to do with them being successful and Joe and Paul just wanting to carry on and keep on rocking and rolling and not caring about the money and not buying things, whereas Mick wanted to buy a nice house and a nice car, he got a girlfriend who was a model, he started living the Pop star life they were making fun of and so that became sort of dangerous. And they - Joe and Paul - felt that it was sort of dangerous that they didn't become the sort of Rock'n'Roll assholes they were rebelling against so - it had a lot to do with that, although I would never call Mick Jones a Rock'n'Roll asshole. He was just young and wanted to have fun and wanted nice things and Joe and Paul didn't care about nice things...

Ray Jordan: As they got famous people started- it wasn't like in the old days when you were trying to get there. Now they had it, everybody started taking liberties, you know? This one's girlfriend says she wants this and that and you start going out with different models and it wasn't like that in the beginning.

JOE VS SUCCESS

Chris Salewicz: I'm absolutely sure Joe was frightened of the success that he got.

Terry Chimes: Oh I think that was the case right from the very first day because we used to argue... I think it was Joe that said, 'We don't want any money' and I said, 'What the hell are you talking about? We don't want any money! Don't be silly!' 'Because', I said, 'if you wanna be successful, the best band in the World - you always wanna be the best band in the World - you gonna sell millions of records and millions of pounds come in so what are you gonna do with it?' You know? You can't have one without the other and I forget how the argument went but it made him uncomfortable looking at those issues. Joe was always uncomfortable being comfortable, he didn't like to relax with money and comfort and that, he always felt he should be fighting a battle and I lost count of how many times I said, 'For God's sake, relax!'

Kris Needs: You have to take into account Joe's own quite fragile psychological make-up. I mean he, he spent his childhood in boarding school, he spent a lot of time wandering about, he was busking, he was part of the London pub scene. He was always trying to find something and then he did with The Clash and he leaped in feet first like he did with everything, I mean he didn't do anything half-heartedly, and the sudden impact and fame and success that The

Clash had, Joe really - he found it rather hard to deal with...

Chris Salewicz: The contradiction of his kind of upbringing, his squatting background, what he was supposed to be, plus money - it's really a complex issue for him 'cause he's a bit naïve as well, Joe is a bit naïve. That's an important point, you know? I mean, he's developed in many ways, creatively, artistically but there's a few basic things he hasn't really figured about life.

Pearl Harbor: He was worried where the band's direction was going... Money shouldn't have worried Joe, he wasn't a big spendthrift or anything and didn't really give a shit about money so I don't think it scared him but he knew that real Punk rockers don't have money and so how are you gonna be this angry rebellious person with money? So he had to figure that out. I think he did a good job of it.

Tymon Dogg: I think Joe was wised up that he could get screwed over but great survivors something like - Dylan's probably one of the greatest survivors of modern culture - and I think it's a question of knowing where you're standing, what you believe in and I don't think success was the problem...

Pat Gilbert: If you're a band and you've got a set of ideals, you're bound to be a bit kind of concerned if suddenly what you're doing is kind of the opposite of what you kind of what you set out and said you were gonna do in the first place.

Chris Salewicz: I think he had a lot of trouble adjusting to all that, although it's odd in a way 'cause obviously this is what he'd been going for all along you know? So there is a little bit of a contradiction there but there's a lot of contradictions and paradox about Joe, there's a lot of contradictions and paradox about The Clash! But as Jung says: 'all great truths must end in paradox'.

Mick Jones: Same time you can have a really great time and not realize you are being relegated, not that we were being relegated but it was becoming too much in a way that we didn't know how to handle all that tension or something, we didn't really know how to handle it all. We hadn't really thought about it when we were going for it, what it would actually be like, we didn't have any plans.

Kris Needs: Some people say during The Who dates that it was the beginning of the end because they suddenly - they'd hit the roof that they were trying to avoid when they were starting - that they play stadiums.

Joe Strummer: To be touring stadiums with them, in a way it was traumatic because it was like seeing where we might end up, 'cause we were sort of supporting The Who and they were pulling the crowd in and I could see that in order to get to that position you'd have to become a travesty of yourself. It really got to me thinking that your whole life would be like doing a photo shoot in the morning, then shooting some crap video in the afternoon and then doing some interview and you'd never... the amount of promotion needed to drive, you know - it would just destroy a person...

STRUMMER/JONES TENSIONS

Mark Helfond: In any decent group there's always tension, that's how it works. No one gets anywhere by being nice to each other because then you just spend all the time in the pub.

Chris Salewicz: I don't know if it was a tension between Mick and Joe but I saw Joe being kinda difficult with all of them, really to be honest. I mean it was Joe who'd always take the contrary line. Sometimes you felt, because he felt that's what he had to do, almost if he didn't quite believe it...

Ray Jordan: Mick can be really laid back and everybody's ready to go but Mick would take about another hour to get to the tour bus, you know, while we're all sitting on the bus then Mick would come along, spliff in mouth, he's ready to go now. Everybody was pissed off about it. Joe he would go specially on his own not to be with Mick. Like he would take a car while everybody else would be on the coach. Joe would take a car and travel on his own 'cause he was pissed off with him just doing his own thing. Never wanting to be on time, he just didn't care, he didn't see the reason why he had to be on time. We all had to wait on Mick, that was going on every day, every night, even to go to the sound-check, to go to the show, to catch a plane, we leave at Mick's time.

David Mingay: I remember Johnny Green saying how he had to go the door, knock on the door and say, 'Mick are you there? I've got your breakfast, I've got your orange juice' and he would say, 'Fuck off!' and then he said, 'No, it's lovely orange juice...' 'Is it the orange juice, freshly pressed?' and then he would say, 'Alright well I'll let you in then, Johnny'.

Jock Scot: It was two camps wasn't it? And you've got Kosmo's influence as well... I think he more or less stamped his flag in the ground at Joe's feet and Mick was looked upon as this camp... you know Rock'n'Roll Star! He was a Rock'n'Roll star! But the Strummer camp didn't like him to make it obvious that he was prepared to enjoy the fruits of their success. I think that's where the split is.

David Mingay: Mick was good at dealing with the music business and he wanted to join it but he didn't see that necessarily as going against his principles...

Pearl Harbor: Joe and Paul were more into being Robin Hoods and everything for the kids and not caring about money and then Mick was more - he had more of a Pop star mentality which was what they were supposed to be rebelling against. So that's how come Joe and Paul were always pissed off at Mick it was like, 'Yeah we just made this bunch of dough, who cares? Put it aside and let's keep going!' But Mick was like, 'No, I wanna get a house and a nice car and go on vacation'. So that was... how I saw it as the beginning of the splitting of the camps was Joe and Paul just wanted to keep plugging, keep - you know - being everything for the kids and all that kind of stuff, and Mick was like, 'Hey we just made some money, we haven't made any money forever, we've been working hard, let's take a break' which is reasonable! But to Joe and Paul and Bernie that was unreasonable...

Jock Scot: They're such different people, you know, Joe was older for a start, only by a few years but that was a big difference I think at that time. Joe was too old to be a Punk Rocker really, because I was the same age as Joe and I certainly felt, these young kids are a bit fucking leery you know? I didn't feel it was my generation's thing at all. And Mick is such a natural Rock'n'Roll star and wanted everything that went with it, all the trappings, he was like: bring it on! And Joe I think, guided by Bernie's sort of left wing political stance, was made to go easy on the fucking flat in Powis Square and thank goodness none of them drove except Joe, did they? So they weren't buying Ferrari's and Lamborghini's or anything. Joe used to drive in an old banger but I can't remember the rest of them ever driving a car. Thank goodness, can you imagine Mick Jones at the wheel?

Tymon Dogg: In a way it was quite a paradox that you had Mick, who from what I know when I met him, was in a tower block and you had Joe from a relatively privileged background, and it was funny how they took on the almost opposite characters to what they really...You see, like Mick was the working class guy and then Joe was sort of trying to cover up his background as if anyone gave a shit basically, you know?

Chris Salewicz: Mick has no problem with having quite a nice, relatively opulent Rock star lifestyle, you know? If he wants to order something on room service when they're on the road, you know a nice meal sent up to his room, he'll do that, but Joe hears about that, he'll hit the roof!

Tymon Dogg: I think Mick was very honest about being in a Rock/Pop band and Joe was never really comfortable from quite early on, there was this whole other agenda going on there which I think he stuck to but if ever he slid out of it he was riddled with self-doubt and guilt so he kind of, on one level, he needed that stuff to keep him what he was, but on the other hand he wanted to be famous and not famous at the same time.

Terry Chimes: They always were very different. That was OK, that's a strength in a way but I think they grew apart on that tour, they grew apart 'cause... I think we were becoming more successful which was making Joe more tense generally and I think Mick was kind of enjoying the success and Joe was feeling more pressure from it and it created more tension between them because - it's hard to explain it really but on stage you'd feel tension between them. On stage you could feel it... sort of grappling with each other without touching each other there was like that kind of tension there. I mean, the tension was good 'cause it made the show! As I said, The Clash was all about tension and conflict and the tension was really strong and it came out and the audience felt it and they enjoyed it (laughs), it's a funny thing. But you can only do it for so long and then it just explodes.

Mick Jones: Yeah, I was out on my own I suppose. I was pretty difficult to get along with 'cause things weren't going my way so I was in a bad mood all the time yeah...

Tymon Dogg: I always find Mick to be a very honest guy. I always had a very straight forward honest relationship with Mick. I've always told him what I thought, you know? Good and bad or what he was doing and I think he was sometimes treated a bit like a - the kind of troublesome child. A child that wasn't happy about something.

Chris Salewicz: There was a famous example on the American *Combat Rock* tour, which Terry Chimes told me where Joe - Mick was doing, you know, playing his guitar hero stuff, with lots of filigree on it and Joe comes over and puts his hands on the strings to stop him, you know? Which Terry saw as a significant moment -

Pearl Harbor: They were for the most part mostly civil to each other. After shows there was a lot of fighting or whatever, I didn't - if they were having band meetings I would disappear, I didn't wanna hear all - what their problems were 'cause I loved them all so I didn't wanna know about the fights.

Mick Gallagher: I think it was a love-hate, I dunno. They were the writing force in the band and they seemed to have an unspoken link with each other and I think the problem was with that, that they drifted apart and as far as I could see, I mean I don't know but as far as I could see Bernie was the wedge between them...

Viv Albertine: The artistic relationship, the intelligence and the respect between them was the very positive beginning of The Clash and probably was the root and the driving force behind The Clash.

Kris Needs: This friction reminded me of Mick Jagger and Keith Richards... you couldn't be more poles apart than their personalities. For a while it worked in The Clash, it gave them an edge, but in the end it drove too big a wedge between them... then there were other factors coming in, like the Bernie Rhodes factor.

Terry Chimes: Towards Christmas... there were serious conversations about what's gonna happen next and this idea came up that Joe and Paul were saying, 'We don't know if Mick is gonna be involved' and that just - actually looking back I didn't take him very seriously, I thought: no, that can't be right, that's silly. I don't know, I found it very odd to imagine The Clash without Mick. I mean, I understood, you know why there were tensions between them and why they were angry at each other, I understood that. But I just didn't see that as an option but they did.

Mick Jones: Wow! No I never knew anything about that. I didn't know. We were going really fast so we didn't have time for reflection at that particular time - you never know anything, you never know what's gonna happen next minute - something could change - I can understand that.

Terry Chimes: I just think right from the start I never really in my heart, I never thought that was ever gonna work. You take Mick out and whatever else you do it's not gonna work. I never got my head beyond that, you know, never saw it to be a possibility. I did say: 'I can't see that happening, that won't work' - but of course that was just one opinion of many.

Kris Needs: I interviewed Mick just before Christmas '82 which would have been his last interview with The Clash that I think he did in this country. There were no indications at all that he was falling out with the band, he was really happy that they had a successful year, they toured with The Who, I mean… whether they should have done that or not, I mean why not? You know... he was very content, he wasn't sort of sitting there slagging them off. The only weird thing that happened was, we were sitting in Mike's Café on Blenheim Crescent

and Mick was facing the door and he
suddenly looked like that and he went,
'There's Paul!' and I looked round and
there was Paul. He was peering through the
window, he was with someone and then he
scooted off and then Mick went, 'Oh, he saw
me and he ran off!' and I thought: oh,
that's a bit weird.

HELL W10

In early 1983 Joe directs a silent movie...

Ray Jordan: I was hanging out with Joe...
He wanted me to play this part and I don't
even know why... he always had a camera
with him, he always wanted to be a director
I suppose. He asked me to be in it - I
thought it was awful, man - we had fun
doing it. Some of it was at the Roundhouse,
mostly around Notting Hill. We was just
having fun really... That was well lost
that movie. We just done it for a bit of
fun, sitting around the Durham Castle pub
and Joe said he was thinking of doing it.

Mick Jones: I was cast as the bad guy and
we just acted out a part.

Pearl Harbor: Mick in the movie was really
great, really funny and you know he's just
his own character you know?

Mick Jones: I did write some music for it.
It was a Hip Hop symphony of the city and I

think he didn't like it very much. And he didn't end up using any music, it was a silent film so he kinda left it like that, he didn't like the music anyway so... then they put it on after that music, it's alright, which is fine... you can have any old music 'cause it's a silent movie isn't it... so I just had a piano playing tan, tan, tan tan taaaa. I thought that would have been good but after they canned my symphonic ambitions... it just pulled us further apart.

Ray Jordan: They were putting up with each other, you understand what I'm saying? It wasn't pally, pally, pally but they knew Joe needed Mick, Mick needed Joe and they were putting up with each other.

Pearl Harbor: They were always trying to be friends and they were friends it's just the dynamics were that Joe and Paul were closer and they thought alike and Mick, Mick was like their Rock'n'Roll buddy, he wasn't quite as tight a brother as the other two. But Mick in the movie was really great, really funny and you know he's just his own character you know?

ENTER PETE HOWARD

Mark Helfond: Terry left 'cause maybe the Rock'n'Roll lifestyle wasn't for him, and you know he had a family and he had other things to pursue.

Terry Chimes: I'd been through a very tough year and I enjoyed it and we did all those things, all this touring in America and so on but at that point I felt that I'd been there and done it. I was meant to be there, it was really good for everyone that I came back and it was good that we did it... but if it was gonna be a completely new band without Mick, it would be a whole new project and I didn't really feel like getting involved in a brand new band.

Joe Strummer: There's a new English bloke on the drums here. He's called Peter Howard.

Pete Howard: I was living in Ladbroke Grove and I used to see Paul walking round there and I knew they were looking for a drummer 'cause I read it in the press and I followed him home and knocked on his door and said, you know as you do when you're young, I wanted the job. But when I asked Paul he said, 'Well we're putting an ad in the paper and you should reply to that anyway,' because I think he obviously wanted to do the fair thing, the decent thing, give everyone the same chance.

Chris Salewicz: Pete Howard's drumming is obviously very different to Topper's and to

Terry Chimes's. He's a bit of a meat and potatoes, sort of John Bonham, pound those drums sort of merchant.

Pete Howard: I was like into Prog Rock – Yes, Genesis, stuff like that and I never told them that in the interview.

Mark Helfond: when we did the auditions there was one really young chap who I thought: yeaaah, come on give it some. Nice, lovely attitude, great drummer, fresh faced, you know, doesn't come with any baggage, anything like that but they picked the guy that came along with the leather jacket on and the dyed hair and he'd been in other corporate groups before.

Pearl Harbor: Pete Howard is a great guy, he's like Terry, and a great drummer but he's no Topper. And he knew it. Pete Howard is a really intelligent guy, he was really intimidated. I was all for him, I was all for anybody to keep the band going, so I liked Pete.

Mick Jones: I liked Pete very much. I wasn't really involved in the audition process by that time, we'd drifted a little bit.

Pete Howard: Paul saw himself as a bit of a mediator you know, he was always trying to get them to speak to each other. There wasn't much tension because they didn't talk. You know, it wasn't much of an atmosphere in the dressing room…it was alright before you went on stage but there wasn't much kinda group hug going on and there wasn't any camaraderie or anything

US FESTIVAL 1983

Joe Strummer: We got a lot of money for the giant US Rock festival, it's got something to do with the guy that invented Apple computers, Steve Wozniak. Anyway, so he must have had a lot of money so he decided to throw a concert, he probably lost his shirt on it –

Pete Howard: I wasn't privy to anything really. I mean, when I was first in it I was paid 300, 400 quid a week, all my bills were paid, you know if I had a problem they would sort it out but I never actually was told anything about anything you know... the money they were getting paid for the US Festival or all of the stuff that you know... and there were so many secrets from me, and from each other, from everyone you know...

Chris Salewicz: Playing the US Festival, yeah The Clash got half a million dollars but Van Halen who topped the bill the next night got a million dollars so you wonder why The Clash aren't getting a million dollars! But I thought what was the great one – the stroke that Bernie pulls about – you know how they're pulling the press conference that they are demanding that the promoters give – you know, a hundred thousand dollars or whatever it is to, you know, the dispossessed of East LA.

Mick Jones: The US Festival? Big, big pressure on us. You know Bernie was like really sloganeering almost trying to use it and just a massive pressure, even more so, apart from that it was a really big gig and it was my last gig and there was a punch up at the end and then Paul jumped in and then it was: Elvis has left the building...

Ray Jordan: Some fight started, don't know even what it was about, we just had to - I think it was trying to come back on stage or something like that. That was it! But I thought that was the easiest half a million you can ever earn!

Chris Salewicz: There was a fight at the end of the show and Mick apparently muscled in very well according to Kosmo. But a friend of mine, Chris Chappel (who was Springsteen's tour manager, maybe he was The Who's tour manager at that point, anyway) he goes running to Bernie to tell him what's going on, this fight... and Bernie said, 'Well anyway, Mick's not long for this group...'.

Pete Howard: When I came back, I stayed in America for about three weeks and they all came back and when I came back nobody had heard anything about anything, nobody knew where anyone was, what anyone was doing... I kept ringing the office like every day and then got bored and then it was twice a week and then I was like: what the fuck? Is this my job or not? Am I the drummer in The Clash or was that the job? I didn't - well I cared, obviously, but I mean interestingly at that time, and I wish I got it, AC/DC were auditioning for a drummer and I saw the advert and went for it and got to the last two in that one and didn't get that which is actually - considering how fucking mental it all became after the US Festival -with hindsight it would have been absolutely golden to have left after the US Festival because everything that happened after that was shit. It was just horrible, every single day.

Show Host: Ladies & gentlemen, your attention please, The Clash have left the building, The Clash have left the building - no need to scream anymore I guess...

Tymon Dogg: I worked with Glyn Johns in 1983 and Gaby was expecting Jaz at the time. And I was in the street in Lancaster Road and I had gone round, met Joe and we went to the café and then we were coming back from the café to go back in the house to discuss these recordings and we met Mick in the street. And he'd never been to Joe's house even though it was just around the corner to his. And I have a slight regret that if I had got Mick involved in that album, if I just had said to him: I really want Mick to play on this album we might have got a no, but there would have been nobody playing games, you know? That was the thing, you see? You don't work with people out of the games, once the games come in, forget it and it slows everything down!

Meanwhile back at Rehearsals Rehearsals...

GOODBYE MICK

Mick Jones: Bernie said let's do New Orleans music and that was like kind of way, I think probably his way to kind of get us back to refocusing but was like - why would we wanna do that, you know what I mean? So that was like, we were not really on good terms by the time we were trying to do New Orleans music in Camden Town, not that I have anything against New Orleans music but it just seemed ridiculous and it was soon after that - then I left.

Chris Salewicz: Well one of the things about Mick that is undeniable is that he's always late! And as we all know when you deal with people who are always late, it can drive you completely crackers! Because it also puts things out of schedule. I think that was a big problem. But - very significantly - on the date he's fired, Mick turns up early and no one's there!

Johnny Green: Hey Mick! You're late, they're waiting in there for you.

Mick Jones: Alright Johnny.

Mick Jones: I was early for once! And so I went up and I thought sod this, 'is anybody else here?' and they went 'no', so I went out the book shop up the road and then I came back and funnily enough Topper was there as well that day and he'd already left the group - just shows you how close we are anyway.

Ray Jordan: Mick just came up to me and he went, 'You're not gonna believe this! They just sacked me from my own band!' and I said, 'You're joking,' and he said, 'Yes, I'm going now'. Went to his guitar case, packed his guitars and gone and Joe looked around and Joe looked at me and went, 'Well that's your boy if you want to, you can go as well, that's your boy - follow him then!' So I just kept quiet 'cause I wanted my job, I just went with the flow because there's no sense following Mick. So that's - but he couldn't believe it, they just told him one day like, 'We don't want you in the band anymore'.

Mick Jones: Basically we were fed up with each other by that time so we - we've had enough and we all got on our own trips, and our own trips were like - it wasn't the same. You know when we were all together at the start? We were like - c'mon guys we can do this you know - blindly going forward and then we did do it, and then we started to fall apart.

Joe Strummer: We had to change the team because the atmosphere was too terrible to - we got so much work to do that we can't waste time begging people to play the damn guitar!

Terry Chimes: Bernie and Kosmo and Paul and Joe all thought, if we do that we solve all these problems, actually yeah, you solve a problem but you throw the baby out with the bathwater because the band is no longer the band it was.

Tymon Dogg: My personal feeling was, just get on with it, have an argument, have a row with Mick over something and sort it out! That's more my way of going round it. That wasn't Joe's. Joe would have Bernie, ta, ta, ta, ta... and then maybe he'd have a row [laughs]. But I just think, you know, any other group probably would have gone, 'God, we can make a killing now!' And they would have gone for the Pound notes or the Dollars - and they didn't, which is made them relatively unique, 'cause I mean, can you imagine U2 squabbling as soon as *Joshua Tree* comes out?

Paul Simonon: At this point we were sort of grown men and you know, as it's been reported, you know Mick did get a bit out of hand in a very - in an Elizabeth Taylor way with his moods and whatever. At the time that's what we felt. We felt we've had enough, let's kick him out and that's what we decided on and to hell with the consequences.

Mick Jones: After a while you work together and you're living in each other's pockets almost continually and in our time we didn't ever have holidays where you have a break so we just continued without any questions... so obviously you get fed up with each other and then the group splits up even though there must have been lots of other reasons you would think contributing towards it... you don't really see it happening at the time because you are going too fast to notice anything and then the next thing you know it's like... car crash.

Paul Simonon: He always wanted holidays and it was terrible because we always wanted to get on and do the job, so we had a tour set up and just about to start the tour, Mick's off on holiday, so obviously we didn't do the tour which is a bit of a pain in the neck.

Mick Jones: They say I didn't want to tour, but I wanted to play some places we hadn't played before or something like that. So it wasn't that I didn't wanna tour, but I wanted to play some other places. They say I didn't wanna tour but I did. But I wanted to play in Eskimo land.

Chris Salewicz: Yes it's the end of August and we were at a party and some girl from CBS, Sony then was, says, 'Mick Jones been fired from The Clash today,' and we couldn't believe it and we tried to ring him in fact from that party but we only got an answer phone. I couldn't believe it! I thought it was complete insanity! He writes the music! Everyone knows he writes the music, this is real madness, it's really crackers! No one's thought this one out I thought.

Viv Albertine: Firing Mick from his own band is absolutely insane. You know, they had no right to fire Mick, you know it's either: do you want The Clash to disband or do you want whatever but you don't fire Mick from his own band, he *was* The Clash, you know? Whatever Bernie thinks and whatever Joe thought, Mick was The Clash.

Jock Scot: Well I think everyone was surprised, even though there had been warning signs that all was not well, I was really shocked and not that, you know it wasn't, 'It's the end of the World!', it was like, 'Why have they done that? He's the musician!' You know, Topper and Mick were the musicians, Joe wasn't a musician... he could strum a few chords... Joe Strummer! Strums a few chords!

Nick Sheppard: They lost a good half of the band, a GOOD half of the band. There's a story about Mick drawing a line in the rehearsal room saying, 'You and Paul, you're the performers, over this side we're the musicians!' so in a sense yeah, they lost the musicians.

Mickey Gallagher: I couldn't understand it, it was beyond me you know, why they were doing that. They were such a high flying band and had lot of creativity and it wasn't premeditated creativity, it was just off the cuff, you know what I mean?

Pearl Harbor: I was as sad as everybody but I did see it coming because they were always talking about it, specially Bernie. He was - Bernie and Joe were adamant that - actually Paul was too, because they were so disappointed that he cared more about himself than the image of the band or their fans. Whereas what made Joe and Paul tick and Kosmo and Bernie for that matter was the fans and keeping it, keeping the momentum up and not letting the money spoil things, but Mick let the money spoil things and that's what pissed off the others...

Mickey Gallagher: I thought they were so tight as a four piece, you know? And they didn't really need - management just seemed to screw 'em up. They seemed to have a purpose and a direction all of their own that managers, I don't know, they seemed to put something in their way...

Joe Strummer: The one final thing that made me really go over the edge was that he started going on about his lawyer a lot and saying, 'Well my lawyer says this, my lawyer says that', and I didn't want to that come between us because we're a team you know, we decide what we're gonna do amongst ourselves we don't go and see lawyers about it. What have they got to do with it? And when he started to say, 'Well my lawyer... you can sign that publishing deal if my lawyer says it's OK, or do this if my lawyer...'. I just said, 'Go write songs with your lawyer'.

Jock Scot: Rock'n'Roll history is lesser with errors isn't? But that is one that leaps out as a mistake of poor management. I mean who was managing the Clash when the decision was made to sack Mick Jones? Bernie!

Kris Needs: There was a time in July 1978, when Mick was getting quite into the - you know, sort of cocaine superstar lifestyle for a brief time, he sorted himself out. But just during that little period they were thinking of getting Steve Jones in from the Sex Pistols because Mick was being a bit of a prima donna... I was shocked when they sacked Mick! But Joe by this time was, actually I don't think any other member of the band was relevant at that point apart from Bernie! 'cause Bernie had a hold on him. Asking Bernie back meant that he had his band back, and Joe was very easily influenced by stronger personalities, and Bernie was like a father figure.

Viv Albertine: The relationship between Joe and Bernie became closer, definitely and you know, I see Mick as the driving force behind the band, I see Mick as a very honest person, a very talented person, a very beautiful person and Joe siding with Bernie really just exaggerated probably the negative sides in both their personalities because Joe wasn't probably quite as sincere a person as Mick, and Bernie certainly isn't a particular sincere person, so to have double dose of that when those two sided together, you know it was just unbalancing in the band really and Mick was on his own and I'm not saying Mick is any saint but he is actually a true person, a true and honest person and the other two have many agendas.

Tymon Dogg: Oh yeah, completely and everybody had their own agenda. Mick had his own agenda, Joe had his own agenda, everybody has their own agenda. I don't see what's the matter with that! Because how do we know what other people's agendas are?

Mike Laye: I think Bernie was very close to Joe and very influential on Joe and I think Mick, like me, was a little bit more suspicious of Bernie and where he was taking everything and where he was going.

Chris Salewicz: Mick's not naïve, you know, Mick is not naïve that's the point and Joe is a bit naïve. And possibly Paul is at that stage as well, I'm not sure actually. But Joe is certainly a bit naïve and seems to need a father figure like Bernie. Often the role of managers, of course. And that's really the hold that Bernie had on him.

Vic Godard: When he spoke to The Clash it was always Mick who was the one he sort of found he was the one that spoke back to him.

Mick Jones: Let Bernie sort out those damn...

Vic Godard: The others tended to sort of like more agree with him whereas Mick was more of a sort of... more of a strong individual.

Mick Jones: Don't tell me to shut my mouth!

Jock Scot: I think Joe leaned heavily on Bernie, just to make sense of the madness that was occurring more and more. As it does, you know, it's not real all that stuff that happens to people like Joe Strummer when The Clash becomes a brand and it goes Worldwide. Everything is different and you need someone from the beginning that you can talk to. Someone who knew you before you were Joe Strummer, World famous.

Mickey Gallagher: It occurred to me that sometimes you had Joe Strummer who was the icon, the positive leader, and at the same time you had this other person within who was called John Mellor who seemed to be a little bit frightened of life and needed people like Bernie.

Jock Scot: I think Bernie would have been saying to Joe, 'We'll lose Jones, we'll get two other guys and we won't have the problem that Mick has become,' and Bernie's eyes - Bernard's eyes - Yeah, I think Mick's shabby sacking... was you know, I'm sure Kosmo had a word about it. Would surprise me that he would have not put his foot down but he probably sided with Joe and Bernie and said right, we can lose Jones and we'll go on without him. But with the benefit of hindsight obviously, that was a mistake.

Mike Laye: I just didn't understand why it would happen and I said to Bernie, 'Did you try and stop him?' And he said, 'No, we're gonna reinvigorate the band it's gonna be a new thing, we're gonna go forward, we're not looking backwards.'

Nick Sheppard: I'll tell you a funny story about Mick getting fired. Me and my girlfriend went out for a drink, she lived in Holland Park, we went to the nearest pub, and Joe, Kosmo and Bernie walk into the pub and my girlfriend knew Bernie very well. I went up to get my girlfriend a beer, Joe and Kosmo were at the bar, Kosmo is saying to Joe, 'He's gotta go!' And Joe's nodding and Kosmo's saying, 'He's gotta go, he's gotta go!' I didn't know what they were talking about so when I heard that Mick had been fired I kinda went: oh, that's what they were talking about.

Chris Townsend: The inside story was that Mick had grown out of the band, he wanted to do his own thing, which I can understand, he's a very talented artistic person.

Joe Strummer: I just felt that he wanted to go on and do other things so eventually I had to give him a push in that direction...

Pete Howard: Joe rang me and said, 'I got rid of that wanker, are you with me or are you with him?' I wasn't aware that there was a choice on the table, so he said, 'Get down here now, we are going for a drink!' And, after Mick, there was a lot of kinda bonding stuff going on, there was a lot of getting very drunk and we went to Lisbon, me, Kosmo, Joe and Paul, literally three days later, we went to Lisbon and had a really good time.

GUITAR REPLACEMENT #1: NICK SHEPPARD

Nick Sheppard: The first audition was up in Camden, in the Electric Ballroom and there were about sixty other guitar players there.

Nick Sheppard: Before the first audition I went to the pub next door to the hall we played in and it was full of guys with guitar cases nervously drinking half pints of bitter and one guy - you know, we're all looking at each other going, 'Are you going for the audition?' 'Yeah, yeah'... And one guy said to me, 'Oh, do you know who is it for?' And I said, 'Yeah'. You know, I didn't realize it was secret and I said, 'Yeah it's for The Clash.' And immediately half the bar got up and walked out...

Pearl Harbor: Everyone who had to replace Mick Jones or Topper knew that they were – you know had a tough road ahead of them and they were all very intimidated.

Nick Sheppard: I went to the Electric Ballroom with God knows how many – five hundred other guitar players... whatever. Big line of people snaking around the dance floor to go up to the stage to play along to a tape... then there was a second audition at Rehearsals Rehearsals more of the same playing along to a tape and they were kind of – it was, 'Oh you know, this could be for a variety of projects', and I actually said to Kosmo, 'Well if it's not for The Clash I'm not really interested'. I was quite confident during the whole process. I was pretty confident that I was a good pick for the job – 'cause I was! You know, I was the right kind of person... obviously, 'cause I got the job!

Pearl Harbor: I remember Nick Sheppard when he came, I was thinking – great looking, had the style, he played well. He wasn't a brilliant guitar player so it took two of them as everybody says, it took two people to replace Mick, which it did. I mean Vince White and Nick Sheppard are great guys and great guitar players but they're no Mick Jones.

Nick Sheppard: I'm guessing that what they were looking for was what I did and I know Joe said to me early on it's really hard to find a Rock'n'Roll guitar player. So I'm guessing that I got the job because I could play and I had the right kind of set of credentials if you like. You know - I guess I looked right, I guess that's important. You wouldn't want a hippie, you wouldn't want a guy with a beard and long hair. I was like an original Punk, I wasn't a guy that latched on to it as a fan. I was a guy that was playing in a band in 1976 you know and that was making records in 1977. So my influences were the same as theirs...

WILD GUITAR WANTED! INTRODUCING VINCE WHITE

Joe Strummer: Hundreds of people out there would give their right arm to play in The Clash and that's where Vince and Nick came in.

Vince White: I took a day of work and went up there to you know audition for a band, I don't know. I was just quite drunk - extremely drunk!

Nick Sheppard: I was put in a room with the four other guys to learn a bunch of songs and then about five or six weeks in they said, 'Oh, and there's another guitar player coming, he's coming in today'. No warning, nothing. So that was a bit of a shock.

Pete Howard: I wasn't asked what I thought, it didn't matter what I thought, I was next to the roadies really - although forbidden to mix with the roadies.

Vince White: Yeah, I thought I was going to be the main guy so there was a bit of conflict there you know. We both thought who's going to be... who's going to be the one?

Nick Sheppard: Oh, another guitar player, you mean you're not gonna play guitar Joe? Your name is Strummer! What's going on? You know? So he was explaining to me, you know... new look, new idea... two guitarist means that it isn't one person replacing Mick, etcetera.

Pete Howard: I know that Nick loves Keith Richards, he loves Soul. He can do all the moves, he can play like a black Soul guitarist, he's fucking great. And I can tell you how he plays and what he wants to do but I couldn't honestly tell you what Vince - what his heroes were, what his style was, what sound he wanted.

Chris Salewicz: Well I think Vince White is not a bad guitar player actually... but the fact is that before they had one guitar player called Mick Jones and they've gotta get two blokes to try and replace him. I think that's quite significant.

Pete Howard: I don't know what Vince likes musically because he didn't discuss things musically and you know Vince now and again when there was no one looking would play the chords from a Yes song or from a Genesis song just to kinda - it was kinda winking at me that he knew, it was kinda: yeah, I know… But that was as much as I ever got from him musically, I mean you couldn't really talk about music in any kind of open way, you really couldn't. I remember being absolutely vilified for having a Van Halen cassette... yeah, right...

Mike Laye: They seemed to me to be the wrong choice at that time because what Bernie was saying was that it was gonna reinvigorate The Clash, looking at it, I didn't see how you were gonna reinvigorate it by bringing in people who were already enamored by it; because all you were gonna do was reproduce what was going on before and I just got very suspicious at that point about what the band was gonna do. I couldn't see how it was gonna break new ground...

Jock Scot: Nick Sheppard was great, he was the part but Vince Nigel Zero I thought they could have done without. But fair enough, you know they kept going but I they should have called it Clash Mark II or Clash Rehashed or something because for me it wasn't The Clash at all...

Vince White: It's just *Spinal Tap* man, you just turn it up and just fucking whaaam'. That's what I did!

Nick Sheppard: Did Vince have a bad attitude? Vince was hired for his attitude!

Pete Howard: I went down to the audition and Vince was the only person who stood up and said...

Nick Sheppard: In front of all the other guitar players and went, 'This is fucking crap!'...

Pete Howard: 'I'm not fucking playing this shit'.

Nick Sheppard: Oh, he's got attitude...

Pete Howard: And they practically kinda went, 'Right, that's our man'...right there without even really hearing what he was like as a musician.

Nick Sheppard: So they hired him for attitude. What they maybe didn't get was that when you hire someone for attitude, you get their attitude not the one you think you're gonna get.

Pearl Harbor: His personality was different. I mean, you know, just from a friend point of view I found Pete Howard and Nick Sheppard easier to get along with, I hardly ever spoke with Vince, he seemed more a bit stand offish but he had his own issues of insecurity or whatever and I didn't mind it, I just didn't care to hang around him, I was more like interested in people who were funnier.

Pete Howard: which is yet again, yeah sure it's kind of a Bernie Rhodes type thing, you know?

BACK TO BASICS

Pete Howard: When Bernie became more established, once Mick had gone, it was about kind of getting everyone to kind of live rough practically, so my wages went down to practically nothing, there was no means of support… you know obviously there was a great deal of money around you know, but not for me and not for Nick or Vince either.

Chris Salewicz: The new musicians are all on a hundred and fifty quid a week…of course it's a con! But the whole thing it's a con by then isn't it?

Joe Strummer: Even Rock'n'Roll is a con!

Pete Howard: When I stupidly raised the issue and said, 'Look I don't think 100 pounds is a great deal, to be paid to be playing in this'... he'd say something like, 'Look, you are playing with the voice of a generation, the most political front man in the World. Do you really think he would rip you off?' which he said quite compellingly, quite passionately and I'd back down like the Bathonian, the middle class boy that I actually am and kind of thought: well, no shit wish I'd never said now.

Vince White: A hundred Pounds a week? Like I make more money than that by just fucking selling my ass and I make more than a hundred and fifty quid a week, going round the planet making piles and piles and piles of fucking cash for a bunch of people who were supposed to be going around like: oh we're so humanitarian, we love the people, we love... we're so socialist, we love looking after the band and blahdiblah. And they were just cooperated into the bloody system, they'd been taken over, they were cooperated, you know?

Pete Howard: It was all about kind of making life difficult, potentially to make great music.

Vince White: It was like a corporation, and you work... you got your guitar broom and you're walking around, you're sweeping the floor. I've worked in a lot of warehouses and they're all those sort of jobs: crap. And you don't have any say, you don't have a say in anything. You just do what you're told. And you do what you're told to get the money and keep the thing moving along, you know?

Chris Salewicz: Bernie's attitude towards money can be summed up by England's performance at the last Football World Cup… Bernie said, 'You see, men with Bentleys aren't gonna win the World Cup, they should all be on two hundred pounds a week and then money can be put in an account for them for afterwards, when they retire'. But that's very much his attitude towards The Clash.

David Mingay: But it was proven, wasn't it? That when they hit real pay dirt in America they collapsed within months and so Bernie was probably right about that in some respects.

Nick Sheppard: Who was running the show behind the scenes? Well I suppose Bernie, Kosmo… There was obviously an agenda had been set up to deal with the situation that they faced.

Pete Howard: I think because getting rid of Mick had been an either or, it had been Bernie or Mick was the situation, it became Bernie, Kosmo and Joe were basically, you know making the manifesto, choosing the artwork, you know... what we did and didn't do.

Joe Strummer: I don't deal with this drug related culture anymore, it's all Hippie stuff.

Chris Salewicz: Bernie may have said there was a no drug policy but Joe was smoking spliffs all the time! (Laughs) I mean, come on! Maybe a couple of days...

Pete Howard: And all of a sudden no one was allowed to get stoned, nobody was allowed to take drugs, it was a real kinda regime going on about what people could or could not wear, you know... and it was pretty bad.

Chris Salewicz: It's basically business as usual, and the anti-drug thing really – that's a kind of back handed way of criticizing Mick who everyone knows is a big spliff head, of course... but so is Joe – just as much!

Dan Donovan: There was a lot of slagging and public stuff going on from their side and Mick never said a bloody word, which I thought was really cool actually.

Pete Howard: I think Mick was a lot cooler than anybody actually cared to admit...

Jock Scot: I didn't like what they were starting to wear. They were starting to wear Kensington Market, La Rocka sort of commercially produced Punk outfits, you know? And when Joe got the Mohican haircut I just laughed out loud. That was ridiculous, that was like me getting a Mohican... forget it! But I think Kosmo had bigged-up this theory that they would be THE Punk rockers, you know… King Punks and that they would take it back to basics almost. Because there were a lot of bands who sort of paraded the Punk Rock ethos and were playing to huge crowds like The Anti-Nowhere League and all that load of toffee.

Mike Laye: When they turned up with the band, Joe had suddenly got this bright orange Mohican - not exactly a Mohican but short on the side and high on top - bright orange! Really bright orange and it just looked like, it just looked like a desperate attempt to kind of - make Joe modern or something. I mean it just did not sit right with me at all, I just couldn't... that was a moment in which I felt that Joe was being exploited, I felt, I felt... that he was being... that The Clash was being pushed forward for other reasons.

Jock Scot: But I can see why it happened, I think it mainly happened not just for Bernie's political reasons but for financial reasons as well 'cause it had become a monster, there was a lot of outgoings. You know, to pay for equipment and storage and the huge trucks that were moving the equipment around and all that and more and more people started appearing who were sort of, that were supposedly on the firm. It all had to be paid for.

Joe Strummer: We wanted to strip it down back to Punk Rock and see where it progresses from there...

Pearl Harbor: Well obviously it didn't really work very well. That was Bernie's idea but… Mick wasn't there and Mick and Topper were the two people who really made the music different. Paul and Joe's taste and style of writing and playing music was much more simple so Bernie was working with Joe and Paul on music he was probably saying: well get back to basics because that's what you guys do the best.

Nick Sheppard: I think going back to '77 was pretty much the only thing we could have done ... you know we had fifty songs to learn or something, I don't know how many. Two and a half hour sets that we were doing. We had to get the stuff up and running quickly, we were playing by I think late January and I joined in October so we had a lot to do in a short period of time so we couldn't be clever. So yeah it was the only option and it was a good one too, you know? It sounded good.

Joe Strummer: I just feel like the blander the rest of the music is getting the more it needs for something that's raw again.

Jock Scot: Look at what Mick Jones went and did. He did something that was forward from The Clash and look at what The Clash did after Mick Jones left! I prefer what Mick Jones does personally, I think it was far superior and more in touch with the times and what was going on. You know, nostalgia is great but not nostalgia for something you did five years ago, that's crazy!

Chris Salewicz: The trouble is that Joe is coming out with all that stuff about going back to basics or whatever but if you look at him, the state of his soul is fairly evident and you don't really necessarily believe what he's saying in those interviews. Actually, you're not convinced that he's convinced.

Joe Strummer: Punk was a rebellion against self-indulgence, Punk said, 'To Hell with self-indulgence!'

Chris Salewicz: He seems to be actually behaving like a dictator to be honest. And he also seems extremely angry. And sometimes you think it's this contrived anger… for the sake of the media? But actually, I think he's imploding with anger...

Joe Strummer: The message is: now is the time to cut everything out that's been wasting all your time...

OUT OF CONTROL...

KOSMO: IF YOU WANT TO BE OUT OF CONTROL!!! NOW IT'S THE TIME!!! IT'S THE CLASH!

Joe Strummer: For so many years you've been with just four people down the road and then here's complete strangers coming in. It was scary but it was much more fun than I thought it would be.

Nick Sheppard: We started playing in America. Big gigs, fifteen thousand people, Stadium Rock, you know? Songs they knew, they all had a great time. We got reviewed in America reasonably well and they gave us space but we got slammed by the English press straight away as I remember.

Joe Strummer: We put together a new unit and we went out and at first it was scary 'cause you think like are we gonna play a bad gig? Can we do it? And we started knocking off a few good shows you know, it felt really great...

Mick Jones: I did try to phone up all the promoters in the World and told them I was coming out with The Clash as well just to mess with them a bit... but apart from that I was fine with it, I was only kidding.

Pete Howard: How fucking *Spinal Tap* is that? It's just fantastic. I mean I was aware of it slightly but I mean I just think it was kind of a pure irony.

Mick Jones: It was a complete wind up just to make Bernie go crazy.

Nick Sheppard: Mick and Topper's 'real Clash' was talked about, never happened. Injunctions being slapped on, gigs were talked about, it didn't make any difference, we still played, we still called ourselves The Clash.

Nick Sheppard: Touring America, you're 24, you're single, everybody loves you, everybody wants to take you out and show you the town, buy you drinks... geez! What a hard job! What a terrible life... it was fantastic! I loved it... it was hard work, it is hard work, we were playing two and a half hour sets and then doing encores and you know? Then getting on the bus sometimes and travelling overnight. Or getting up early in the morning and travelling all day. So there was a lot of sleeping on the bus though but I loved it… even though there were the occasional kind of horrendous rows and flare ups... I just thought: what a great job!

Pete Howard: I don't think we flew, hardly at all and we were driving massive drives and I don't think there was a toilet on the bus and it was uncomfortable, you know what Greyhound buses are like, they're for poor people you know? But as I say it was another example of: 'if you give 'em any comforts then they'll become shit' but to be honest I think it was shit anyway and his idea wasn't getting us any better, you know?

Pearl Harbor: It wasn't as much fun as the early Clash tours definitely, everybody tried and specially Joe and Paul were trying to make it work and have a successful band but it was just very, very difficult. It's hard to replace people, it's hard to replace your youth, all that. You can't have money and pretend that you don't, you know all that stuff goes into the Punk Rock picture, it doesn't go into every Rock'n'Roll story but it goes into Punk Rock because Punk Rock is supposed to mean a certain thing, you know what I mean? It's supposed to mean youth and rebellion. So when you have money and you're no longer youthful it's a little bit difficul...no disrespect to the guys.

Chris Salewicz: They were sort of OK, you know it was alright... sort of. Sort of. They weren't awful, they really weren't awful but it wasn't The Clash as I knew it. Obviously Joe was still pretty good, Paul seemed to be throwing more shapes than ever and the new blokes weren't really lit. And it was sort of alright, they got away with it.

Jock Scot: Nick Sheppard and Joe and another one had big ears and when there was light coming from behind you'd see these sort of big ears and they did look like three European Cups in a row.

Pete Howard: It wasn't very fucking good, it wasn't a good band anymore. You know, they did the moves and stuff and you're hearing the songs you want to hear but there wasn't a focus and nobody really knew what they were doing. And as I say, because everyone was so scared of doing the wrong thing you actually end up behaving abnormally you know?

Jock Scot: I didn't like the look of the Vince Nigel, I thought he looked a bit spotty for the group. I thought Nick Sheppard did very well in a difficult sort of situation and apparently they played some great gigs, specially in America. I think the British public, specially the early fans, had rumbled that this was not good, that something smells funny about that.

Mick Jones: Pete was a good guy and you know as it must been, consequently the group after I left, he must found it very difficult circumstances, and it's very difficult if you're not actually emotionally connected to the songs that you're playing as well, if you haven't lived the songs, how difficult it must be to try to play them and sing them without any conviction so I felt for all those guys.

Ray Jordan: Bernie Rhodes thought, you know, well there's some more guys he can tell what to do, so he had full control. Joe sort of decided to let Bernie do whatever he wanted. But Paul didn't say much. He was happy just to stand there and follow Joe. But those guys - I felt really sorry for them 'cause they couldn't handle it. And you know, two guys to play Mick's part? And not only that but the audience would tell them they're no Mick Jones and the times they... you could see them crumbling on stage, they tried their best man, but no way they could have handled it.

Rudy Fernandez: I felt sorry for them, you know? I mean they were great guys but you can never do that. It was like replacing Pelé on a soccer team, you know? You could never do that, it was a no win situation for those guys. And I used to tell them, 'Enjoy it while you can guys!'

Pearl Harbor: They were just playing the songs. Mick used to play different solos all the time, he used to add things or throw something away but these guys, it was just like going through the motions. It wasn't their fault, they just to me weren't as exciting. But they were good and they served their purpose, they were rebels, Rock'n'Roll rebels...Paul and Joe wanted to continue with the tough rebel posse...they were fine.

JOE HITS ROCK BOTTOM

Nick Sheppard: I'm not gonna comment on someone's personal life but I've had kids and I've lost my dad, I know how hard losing a parent is and I know how hard leaving your children is - Joe had both those things happen during the first six months I was in the band so I'm not gonna comment on how he felt but I can imagine.

Chris Salewicz: Joe's dad passes on in the autumn of 1984 while they're on, you know, the dodgy Clash tour of Britain and he just goes to the funeral. Leaves to go to a gig that night, he doesn't have any time to mourn it and for what I understand no one in the rest of the group is told about it.

Pete Howard: He disappeared for two days and we didn't even know he had gone to his father's funeral. We didn't know why he had gone anywhere and it came out in one of Bernie's - someone said something about not being particularly happy about something and Bernie was like, 'Look, this guy just buried his father and you're talking about...' whatever you were talking about. And I didn't know his mother had cancer, I knew nothing about it, nobody did. I don't know if they saw that as being kinda stoic you know that they weren't telling the troops the bad news.

Chris Salewicz: Then at the same time his mother is ill, she's got cancer. She's in the hospice, he's going to visit her regularly. He's been in a crisis really ever since Mick's kicked out of the group, but it's like... there's a succession of kind of plunging ravines that he's crashing down...

Kris Needs: When he started having some personal problems going on, you know family stuff... there was a lot of turmoil, he was quite ripe to be steered by Bernie, it's what I'm saying, he was quite vulnerable. Very strong guy but very vulnerable, he must have felt that he was taking over the World with Bernie.

BOOTCAMP CLASH

Pat Gilbert: Bernie ran the band like it was some military operation, only kind of not more like a sort of student revolutionary May 1968 Paris' riots operation and I mean, the whole thing is so contradictory and fucked up, you know, but that's why it was glorious you know? Who in their right mind would have Bernie as their manager? Well, The Clash weren't in their right mind...

Pete Howard: They were doing kinda Year Zero stuff, they weren't doing kinda... anything intellectual or even vaguely intellectual, you know reading or talking about a movie it was kinda seen as not that useful, not very helpful, you know... unless it was you know, *The Harder They*

Come or something but if you talked about a French film they would be like: shut the fuck up!

Nick Sheppard: Bernie, Joe and Kosmo obviously had an agenda and Bernie wanted that agenda to proceed and he would use what he thought were the appropriate tactics to get a result. And those tactics seemed along the lines of some weird religion, where you break people down to nothing and then build them up, that kind of exegesis crap. That seemed to be where he was coming from so I suppose, simplistically, that's bullying.

Pete Howard: We had a lot of band meetings all the time and there'd be a lot of, 'And you,' (points with his finger) you know, 'And you... you wear a checked shirt, what fucking band do you think this is? Big Country?'.

Pearl Harbor: Bernie and Joe, if Joe was in a playful mood he loved to bully people. Kosmo, Joe and Bernie all did their amount of bullying but Vince is probably a lot more sensitive to it, he might have taken it a lot more personally.

Vince White: I was bullied from the day one! God - for fuck's sake. The guy fucking was laying it unto me from the day I joined almost.

Ray Jordan: Controlling them, telling them who's the boss. He's the boss, do what I say. That sort of thing but I wouldn't call that bullying, just thought he wanted them to get on with it and don't slack.

Nick Sheppard: Calling Bernie's managerial style bullying it's a bit simplistic. It's not entirely inaccurate but it's a bit simplistic.

Chris Salewicz: There seems to have been a lot of bullying, a lot character assassinations, and just ways of tripping people up psychologically to keep them psychologically unstable... It's not gonna work, is it?

Vince White: The band was a band for about four weeks, and then Bernie jumped in and started kicking... kicking butt and pushing our fucking asses and that was the end of that. You just like become slaves to The Clash machine.

Pete Howard: No one was spared you know? It wasn't just Vince, I think Vince's reactions were worse than anyone else's. I think he took it far more personally in some circumstances than anyone else and I think...

Pearl Harbor: So if any of them caught on to the fact that he was you know, taking it more to heart than anyone else, well then he would have got targeted even heavier because that would have meant that he was a bit soft. Whereas everybody else, the crew, everybody... you could bully anybody and they'd give it right back to you, so if you bullied Vince and he took it personally well they would think: aaahahah you know like that, instead of... they wouldn't let up, they were relentless in trying to annoy him and everybody, trying to get a raise out of them.

Pete Howard: I would disagree so much with what was going on and that was really the problem I think, for me in that situation and I think Vince as well suffered from the same kind of... you know, he couldn't keep his mouth shut and he would sound a lot stroppier than I would a lot of the times 'cause he was going about everything, you know?

Nick Sheppard: I don't think Vince was any more targeted than anybody else and I don't think that Bernie succeeded with what he was trying to do with any of us.

Pete Howard: I know what they were trying to do and perhaps, I don't want to be too positive about anything Bernie did, but perhaps in some kinda way it wasn't a terrible idea to try and get five people to work and bond, you know and make them into a gang.

Chris Salewicz: I mean, this sort of lab experiment, it might be a good idea for a few weeks but it's not a sustainable way of nurturing a creative situation at all! So obviously it's just gonna generate resentment.

Pete Howard: I stood up to Bernie on a number of occasions. I left, went back to the hotel once when we were in America, and packed and had a cab booked… And when Bernie rushed back to the hotel 'cause he realized what shit he may have caused if I actually did go, that was the one and only time he spoke to me in a way that I could hear...

Pete Howard: Even Paul, who was the real fucking deal, he was the genuine article, even he was subject to this witch hunting, McCarthy bullshit if there was ever a glimpse of him doing anything that wasn't completely within the brief.. and you couldn't get anything more The Clash in image and ideas than Paul. He was the real thing you know?

Pete Howard: I would have much rather been sacked or I would have much rather left, rather than suffer all the indignities. But when you're in one of the biggest bands in the World and you're touring and there's glamour around it then there's your reason to stay amongst it but it's a weak reason, it's not something I can never feel reconciled with I think.

GRANADA

Chris Salewicz: In October 1984, Joe goes down to Granada, in Spain. It's kind of a bit of a pilgrimage for him, he needs to get away from things, he needs a creative place to think.

Jesús Arias: He was in crisis with The Clash, he was trying to put the band together with new members and he came to Granada to think, to relax, and wanted to find Lorca's grave, Garcia Lorca...

Chris Salewicz: He wanted to visit the grave of Federico Garcia Lorca, the great surrealist poet, dramatist who was murdered in the Spanish Civil War and you know, on the road, Joe - one of the things that The old Clash would often be doing was reading books about the Spanish Civil War. So would Mick actually, both of them. They were fascinated by it.

Jesús Arias: He was apparently fine...Lorca, blah, blah... but when you started talking to him in a serious way he was really sad, he was in crisis.

Chris Salewicz: But in fact he doesn't get around to go to the grave that time (laughs), 'cause he sort of meets people. Meets this group called 091, Spanish group he wants to produce and he does actually produce about a year later, in fact, which is not necessarily a happy state of affairs.

Jesús Arias: He used to say, 'I'm a shit man, I did nothing interesting in my life', and it was shocking for me because, man you are Joe Strummer! You are like Mick Jagger or...but he wasn't happy at the time. He used to cry a lot for anything, he was really emotional, very... anything could touch him.

Jesús Arias: He said he had to fire Mick Jones because Mick Jones smoked too much dope, too many joints... and he was saying that while he was preparing a joint! Then he said that Mick Jones had become like a Rock star and that The Clash weren't Rock stars, and he didn't want to be a Rock star.

FROM MUNICH TO RICHMOND

Nick Sheppard: We finished the American tour and we came home and there was kinda some time off and obviously the next job was to make a record. And we presumed that we would start thinking about making a record and I guess Joe's phone call about not being on the record was the first time I realized that this wasn't a band as - this wasn't the kind of band that I was used to being in. Joe's phone call was the first time I realized: oh, I don't have any control over this. So I wasn't very happy about it.

Nick Sheppard: So the first idea was - it would be Joe, Norman Watt-Roy, Pete, and I think Mickey Gallagher. So Norman and Mickey from The Blockheads.

Mickey Gallagher: We got together with Joe to do a bit of jamming in the studio in Camden and I was playing a Hammond, Joe wanted me to play a Hammond but when we went and listened to it and it sounded a bit Dylanish, you know? So Bernie was in the control room and he wanted to change it, make it different so he put the organ out of phase with everything else. So I walked in the studio and I went, 'What's going on? What's going on?' And he was just, 'Just trying to make it different…' 'Make it different?' I said. 'It sounds terrible, it's all out of sequence with everything else!' He said, 'It won't be like that when it's finished', you know?

Nick Sheppard: I heard them rehearsing and they sounded bloody awful. They sounded like Pub Rock, it sounded awful. So that didn't happen, and so demos were done with Joe and Michael Fayney who ran the studio and I played on some of them and suddenly I was on the record again!

Mickey Gallagher: And that was the last I heard, when I did that session, I didn't get asked back, so you know - I just took it that he didn't like it and Joe was doing everything Bernie said at the time...

Norman Watt-Roy: Yeah, that was the kind of thing I noticed when I went out to Munich with Joe. Joe changed when he was around

Bernie, he was kind of like, 'yes Sir, no Sir' to Bernie.

Nick Sheppard: I don't think Joe became a Yes man to Bernie. I think that he decided on a course of action to take with Bernie, without realizing Bernie's ulterior motive which was to become a member of The Clash. And I think by the time we got to make the record he had realized that that was going on and it didn't sit well with him. But it was too late to go back. He had to believe in what he was doing and he told me that. He said to me in Munich, 'I have to believe that this is the right thing to do'.

Chris Salewicz: Joe deduces that Bernie Rhodes, having seen the success that Malcolm McLaren has had - actually globally! - with records like *Buffalo Gals* and the Duck thing [Duck rock]... Wants yet again to emulate his former partner and become a star himself!

Fayney: The decision was taken that they would use this producer called '*José Unidos*'... who didn't actually exist! It was basically Bernie Rhodes... and Joe.

Nick Sheppard: I wasn't surprised that Bernie was producing the record - he's a megalomaniac! He wanted to be in The Clash.

Kris Needs: Once Mick had gone that took the music out of the band and who was gonna do it now? Bernie? With his drum machine? You know?

'Joe wanted to compete with Mick's drum machine thing', Bernie Rhodes 2010.

Pete Howard: I was never privy to the conversation about using a drum machine on it and getting Fayney to program the drums in an attempt to make it more contemporary... I don't know, I mean I have no idea what the actual reasoning behind all of that was but obviously I was led to believe it was because I wasn't good enough...

Norman Watt-Roy: I made a big thing saying, 'I don't like these drum machines', I used to be like ... the live drum is much better ...

Fayney: The new Clash album was actually an electronic album. I did the majority of the drum programming on it. And it was supposed, it was supposed to be a new departure. It was supposed to be a fresher, newer, bolder Clash. That's what it was meant to be.

Pat Gilbert: I mean the whole recordings, that's a farce, you know? The band aren't on it so it's done in different sessions... You got session musicians playing on it, the songs aren't very good.

Pete Howard: The only thing I ever did was to sit in the drum booth with the track and get told to play 'like I was throwing the drumkit down the stairs' or... yeah. Or, 'Just do what you want'... 'no, not that', 'no, not that either'. So, you know, it wasn't a very enjoyable session.

Nick Sheppard: Paul Simonon didn't play on a lot of Clash recordings. I think that's common knowledge so I wasn't surprised that he wasn't in Munich to play the bass, no.

Pearl Harbor: I personally thought that it was all unnecessary and kind of ridiculous, you know... why have Norman play bass on most of the songs? Paul is an excellent bass player and he's the fucking coolest bass player on Earth according to their fans, so what's the problem?

Pete Howard: The thing with Paul is that he was considered to have this anchor style, he was an anchorman style icon but nobody was ever vaguely polite about his playing, you know.

Mick Jones: Paul is a fantastic bass player, fantastic bass player, second to none! Incredible. He's not only just the bass... he's more than the bass.

Norman Watt-Roy: Joe came round my yard and he said, 'Hey, I'm making a new album, will you come around to Munich with me?' And I said yeah. I went out there and I didn't really know Bernie, first time I met him was out there and he was producing it, I didn't question it, I just let it go, you know? I thought Fayney was producing it more, really, in the studio, he was more.... doing it more. But I enjoyed it, it was good fun, you know? But it wasn't The Clash! It wasn't really The Clash, it was Joe trying to keep the thing going on his own!

Fayney: He was obviously under an immense amount of pressure to come up with new material that would fit the vein.

Norman Watt-Roy: He didn't have the people he needed like Mick and other guys to write with him and stuff, he was doing it on his own and he was struggling to try - and he took me out there hoping that that was gonna help and all that, but it was hard work ...

Mickey Gallagher: I think he was confused, he didn't know the right move to make, people were forcing him to make a move...

Norman Watt-Roy: He was struggling to write an album...

Pete Howard: Joe essentially had bought the idea that Bernie was the Malcolm McLaren to us, the person who would stop us being boring... If Bernie had an idea then generally they would act upon it even if it wasn't based on any kind of logic at all, which it frequently wasn't ...

Nick Sheppard: By the time we got to the point of going to Munich to make the record I wasn't surprised by anything Bernie did.

Rudy Fernandez: Well I didn't even know he was a producer! When I first saw him over there doing this I was like, you know... I couldn't believe that he was like a producer ... Well, what else? What's next? You know? He's gonna pick up a guitar?

Pete Howard: Vince was in the same boat as me, we were both kind of left in England

and then called to Munich and we drove from here to Munich basically in a shitty van without any heating and you know, we had no money and all we could do was just get there and then we were holed up in a hotel for weeks on end with nothing to do and then I got called in one night and Bernie starts to ask me to do quite kinda strange, stupid and abstract things and every time I'd say: why? He would just say, 'That's 'cause you're a middle class muso bore, just do as I ask you or fuck off!'

Pearl Harbor: All his ideas for *Cut the Crap* went in one ear and out the other, I just thought it sounded like a lot of shit! But what do I care? If they want to make that album and they were all into it, what can I say? I just wanted Paul to be happy because - it's hard for Paul to be happy when he wasn't playing. He just wanted to get on with it and play so all this experimenting and all that stuff didn't sit too well with him I don't think.

Fayney: It was hard work in the studio, it was harder than I thought it was gonna be because the vibe wasn't there.

Pearl Harbor: I remember going into the studio and singing you know, some big back up vocal with a million other people, some big giant chorus and you know, obviously that was fun.

Chris Townsend: I did backing vocals on two of the songs. When we got to the studio we didn't really see much of them, they - all the band members were probably in the booth and we were in the recording studio and

basically dropping down vocals. So it was
an evening, there was a bit of partying
going on, a bit of drinking...

BUSKING TOUR

Nick Sheppard: The busking tour was a
decision that me and Joe made in Munich at
the end of the recording session after a
conversation with Kosmo about taking the
band and doing something as the band,
reconnecting as a band. Because we hadn't
been a band for virtually a year. We done a
few shows but we'd been really disconnected
and Kosmo felt that we needed to become a
band. So me and Joe went for a walk around
Munich and went, 'Well, why don't we go
busking? Fantastic! So we went busking!'...

Chris Salewicz: They seem to think it was
the best tour they ever did, but there was
an element about it... I remember when I
heard about it, I thought: well, they sort
of would, wouldn't they? It seemed - the
eccentricity seemed a bit obvious. However,
they kinda set off, allegedly with no money
- although Paul had a credit card - they
meet in a pub in North London and they sort
of hitch hike...

Pete Howard: We stood by the side of the
motorway all of us dressed in like leather
jackets, leather jeans and tee shirts with
our hair done nice you know? And

unsurprisingly I got picked up by this incredibly furtive gay salesman who just spent the whole of the drive up to Nottingham asking me if I'd ever sucked a dick! And I was like, 'Man I haven't, we've established that, can I get out here?' You know and he was like, 'No, no it's all fine, it's all completely fine'... and then we all met somewhere under a canal bridge, you know with sort of dripping water and rats, but there weren't any rats... but you know what I mean. And they had guitars and I had a pair of drumsticks and I was supposed to find something to hit which was invariably a dustbin or a plastic chair. That was really good fun, really, really good fun. Really unbelievable and Joe was fearless, absolutely fucking fearless about what he did...

Chris Salewicz: They kind of traverse the country for a bit. A couple of weeks or so and it seems to be quite successful... by the time they get to Scotland, people have heard of this. You know, they're getting quite big crowds! Seven hundred, eight hundred people are turning up to see them.

Pete Howard: It was great 'cause we would hand around the hat and very quickly as soon as people knew who we were, there were thousands of people standing around. We'd hand around the hat and you'd get phone numbers and drugs and money and you know... sexual invitations and stuff and it was all really good fun and we would all stay at someone's flat and we stayed at a squat in Glasgow which was brilliant.

Chris Salewicz: Eventually Joe lost his voice and they basically came back to London much to Bernie's anger who felt they should have kept going much longer. But it did seem to me, I didn't say it, but it seemed to me and a lot of people have said, that it was sort of a success and they enjoyed it, it was probably good fun.

YO TE QUIERO INFINITO

Jesús Arias: Eight months later, he came from Munich I think and he was really frustrated with the new record and said, 'That fucking Bernie Rhodes, I don't want to be his toy anymore'. I asked him, 'What's happening?' And he said, 'The Clash is over, I don't want to know anything about Bernie, the band and no further comment'.

Jesús Arias: He was producing 091 and he was in crisis with the assistant of the company because they wanted to use his name but they didn't want Joe around and they didn't want him to produce 091, they thought he was a drunkard, he didn't go to the studio, blah, blah, blah. So Joe had a crisis, bought a car, a Spanish-American car, a Dodge Dart. He phoned me and he came to Granada and he said, 'Look at my new car man!' He was happy with the car, we were driving through the city and he would say to anyone, 'Hey! Look at my car!' So he said, 'Let's go to Viznar to look for Garcia Lorca's grave'.

Chris Salewicz: He does get to go to Lorca's grave on that occasion and raises a spliff to his memory but also has to be dissuaded from buying shovels to dig, to try and find where Lorca and two thousand other people were executed ... anyway ...

Jesús Arias: So I told him, 'Joe, you're crazy! It's a huge place!' And he said, 'No, no if you and me are here this might be a reason'. He stopped the car, I let him out, I waited in the car 'cause I realized he was a little bit sad so he started walking, smoked a joint. I went out the car and when I reached him he said, 'I can hear them'. 'Hear who?' I said. 'I can hear the scream of the dead, there was a great tragedy here and I can feel it' so he started crying.

LAST SHOWS + THE NASSAU AFFAIR

Nick Sheppard: On the bus to the gig, this is when we played in Roskilde... We were on the bus going to the festival. Bernie was giving it some at the front and I saw Joe give him a look of pure hate. And that was kind of when I first realized that this shit was gonna hit the fan, obviously Joe had stopped believing.

Pete Howard: Athens was a great laugh, we had a really good time there. I had the best time of my life in Roskilde, it's a brilliant festival, I saw some bands that I've never forgotten there, you know? And I think specifically that festival made me realize that it wasn't actually, I didn't have to suffer all the time, everybody else seemed to be having a great fucking time.

Chris Salewicz: So they record *Cut the Crap* at the beginning of 1985 and in July that year, I ran into Joe on the street and he said, 'Come and have a drink with me tonight'. And I went to a place called 192 in Notting Hill and we met there about nine o'clock, had a very good evening, quite pissed. And about midnight he says, 'I've got a big problem. I'll go and have a wazz, I'll come back and tell you about it'. And he sits down and says, 'Mick was right about Bernie' (laughs). Well, actually we could have told you this Joe, you know? But I was amazed, I was really amazed you know? Because this was like a very pivotal moment. Wow!

Chris Salewicz: And he goes round to see Mick and Mick is actually waiting for a cab to take him to the airport 'cause he's finished the first BAD album and he's exhausted, he's going on holiday, he's going to Nassau. And so they have a spliff and then the cab comes after about five minutes. And then the next thing Joe gets on a plane and goes out to Nassau and he doesn't know where he is! And rents a moped, you know, which I think he crashed, and scores a big bag of weed and eventually finds Mick and offers it to him as a penance.

Dan Donovan: When I arrived there, it was about eleven o'clock at night and I turned up at their villa and there was a guy in the swimming pool! He was splashing around in the middle of the night, completely drunk... it was Joe Strummer. And I learned that he'd actually cycled around the island for three days knocking on random doors trying to find Mick because he'd come there with a mission of ask him to reform The Clash. So eventually he found Mick and I think he'd been drinking Rum for four days so he was like a bit pissed, well he was completely pissed basically.

Chris Salewicz: And then Mick plays him the BAD album and Joe, tactful as ever says, 'It's no good! You need me!'... Possibly not the best way to go about it and he suggests to Mick that they get back together but Mick says it's a bit late.

Ray Jordan: Joe came up to me and said what a stupid mistake he made and that he should have never followed Bernie... he was in tears after a time. He just broke down, he knew he had made a mistake but by that time Mick had started Big Audio Dynamite.

Dan Donovan: It was too late! It was too late, BAD had started and all these characters were involved and up and running and it was going. And it was like, there was no way that that was gonna happen... And I could see that Joe, he was in pain at that point. His life had gone out of kilter. He felt massive guilt about breaking up the band... yeah. They felt guilty, I mean him and Paul sacked Mick from his own band! I mean that's insane! You know he started The Clash ... I think Joe did feel guilty and had come there with the express wish of trying to reform it but it was too late, it was way beyond that...

CUT THE CRAP

Pat Gilbert: I tell you a thing about *Cut the Crap*, you gotta put in context of what was happening in Joe's life. I mean, Joe at that time was Bernie's foil. I mean he's the guy who's got the opportunity to take control of this but he was having to deal with pretty bad issues in his private life, I mean his father died and his mum was very ill. I mean his mind was elsewhere and I think he might have been having his kids at that point as well. You know he just let

Bernie take control, maybe he had genuine faith in him that he would do something really radical and great but it proved otherwise.

Mike Laye: I just thought what they should do was just drop the 'Cut' from the title, because to me this was crap. As far as I'm concerned there's only one good song on it, which is 'This Is England' and I thought that was good.

Pearl Harbor: They were excited about it, it was the best song on the record as far as everybody was concerned, it was the only song that was worth anything so they were hoping that it'd be a big success because then it would be a, 'Phew! At least there's a good song off that shitty album'. But I don't remember, I don't think it did that well, but I thought the song was decent.

Barry Scratchy Myers: When *Cut the Crap* came out I listened to it with an open mind but to be honest it was in the title. 'This Is England' was a good song.

Vince White: It's really hard to fucking – it's really depressing because 'This Is England' is such a tremendous song because it represents what's going down! We don't have a fucking England anymore, everything is gone down the tubes...

Mike Laye: But you know, it's not the best song The Clash ever wrote, it sounds like a football anthem and was – you know, it sounded like it might have been done by Big Audio Dynamite as well...

Chris Salewicz: I'm sure they knew the sort of stuff that Mick was doing... I'm sure that they heard, I'm sure it kind of leaked out or not even leaked out, people would have said we're doing this and that and blah, blah, blah... you know?

Mike Laye: I started to feel that this was a band that had outlived its time, that was no longer relevant and was disappearing...

Kris Needs: I heard it when it first came out but I just couldn't stand it, considering the lyrical peaks that Joe had reached on *Combat Rock* I just thought: what's he done? He's turned them into the Angelic Upstarts or something like that. It was just basic sloganeering with none of the subtleties that Joe had built up over the previous few years and all the musical subtlety had gone and you know there was something weird about the production, it had all these kind of electronic instruments on there too, it was just a muddy mess.

Mike Laye: The production was awful. Nobody sounded committed, nobody sounded interested, it was awful, it was awful.

Chris Salewicz: Bernie thinks he's spotted a genre: sort of electro, sort of hip hop, sort of cut-up stuff, and everyone tried very hard with *Cut the Crap* but it's really not very good at all, in fact it's pretty abysmal.

Pete Howard: The idea hadn't worked, the drum machine idea. I don't know what Fayney knew about it, but it didn't exactly swing

like a drum machine does, you know...
that's why you use them! Because they keep
time and you can kinda dance around to them
rather than wondering why someone's hitting
you round the back of the head with a bag
of ball bearings, you know?

Fayney: It wasn't the intention to go in
and make a half-hearted record. We
genuinely wanted to make something that
people would go, 'Wow!'

Terry Chimes: I think I heard it once, I
didn't like it. I quite liked the single, I
thought that was good but the rest of it I
didn't really like and I thought - the
thing is that - Joe and Bernie were the
kind of guys that if you said, 'Let's go
crazy and do something completely off the
wall', they'd go, 'Yeah, let's do it'. But
they needed someone to go, 'Hang on a
minute, well that won't work'... but then
there was no one there to say that 'cause
without Mick there, Mick would have said,
'Well that won't work'. But without him
there they could do something completely
crazy and they wouldn't realize how - what
a mistake it was until it was out in the
shops and - you know - too late.

Pat Gilbert: I think Joe had woken up to
the fact of what was going on long before
the reviews, I think he knew, Joe knew a
good tune when he heard one and there
weren't many on *Cut the Crap*.

Pearl Harbor: I don't really remember like
the bad reviews came out and Joe went, 'Oh
fuck it, I'm out of here'. I don't remember
it like that. I think he pretty much was

disgruntled with the band and the record and then when the bad reviews came out it was probably the final straw.

JOE SPLITS

Joe Strummer: If there was a mistake... I made it!

Chris Salewicz: So it's like November, December '85, it finally disintegrates.

Nick Sheppard: The last band meeting that we had as a group, we went into Joe's house, he said, 'I'm not gonna carry on' and he asked us not to carry on either and we all said that we wouldn't.

Pete Howard: I think by that time, I don't think anyone really could give a fuck, it was just flogging a dead horse. I think when we came back we had this meeting and Joe was kind of like, 'Look we've all made a lot of mistakes here and it's simply not working and all these things that Bernie had told me to do have turned to shit and he was wrong, I admit that he was wrong, I was wrong to have chosen him but I don't think there's anything we can do about it now, it's too late'.

Nick Sheppard: I remember Pete saying, 'You know what you should do is take out a retraction, if you like, in the papers, an open letter, and we should go and record the album as a band', but obviously by the time Joe had called this meeting that wasn't an option as far as he was concerned.

Pete Howard: He wrote this thing which he said he was going to pay for a page in every broadsheet newspaper and all the tabloids to have it printed saying 'Crap Cutting Commencing' with this kind of public broadcast, kind of London Calling... I don't mean the album, I mean the actual kind of wartime broadcast thing, of how the band had basically been hoodwinked by a political dictator... Bernie. It was kind of an apology for every mistake that he was now suddenly aware that had been made, you know? That was kind of yeah, everyone was like, 'God, at least we're all saying it now, at least we can relax about it a little bit'. But obviously he didn't do it (laughs). He didn't do anything with it at all.

Nick Sheppard: But he'd been gone for months before that, he'd been in Spain, unreachable. Bernie used to ring me up every day towards the end, he'd get me out of bed and rant for about half an hour, an hour ... and I said to him one day, 'Bernie, why are you ringing me up every day?' And he said, 'Because I have no one else to talk to'.

Pete Howard: That was the day they met us in Soho... they gave us a thousand pounds in a sweaty envelope and that was that really. That was the end of it, it should have ended considerably earlier than that but... just didn't. I think everybody was very reluctant to let it go.

Kris Needs: Bernie then saw The Clash as a brand; brand Clash which meant that you wouldn't even have to have any members of The Clash in it as long as you had the ideology of The Clash which Bernie had first set out in 1976...

SINGER AUDITIONS

Nick Sheppard: I witnessed the auditions. I actually went to the auditions for new singers because I thought I might find someone that I could work with outside of that situation or maybe as something to do with that situation but not as The Clash.

Pearl Harbor: I know for a fact that Paul would never have been the lead singer of The Clash.

Pearl Harbor: I know that you said that they auditioned different people to be singers of The Clash and I vaguely remember that, but I also vaguely remember that Paul wasn't interested in any of it ... it was more Bernie, and possibly Kosmo, trying to say, 'Look let's keep this going if you want to, do you wanna this or do you wanna do that?' And I think Paul pretty much said no.

Pat Gilbert: Yeah, that's right. Very good, so Bernie gets complete control in the end, yeah, and you know, don't get what you wish for 'cause that's what happens.

Nick Sheppard: I suppose I should say at this time that being in a band like The Clash you're in a situation that is full of extreme contradictions. The Clash were always viewed as a political entity, you know personal politics maybe but as, you know, having something to say, having an agenda and having an opinion but they were also a Pop group. So there's a lot of contradictions going on in there.

Nick Sheppard: The talk of the time with Bernie and Kosmo when we were auditioning for singers and stuff was they were talking about football teams, and about how players left and players came back. That was the kind of rationale that they were using but it was patently bullshit.

Vic Godard: But does he own the name The Clash? He can't do because otherwise he probably would do that, wouldn't he? He'd have a version out there now touring. If he owned the name.

Terry Chimes: I think a band is the people in it, you can change a person maybe and get away with it, you know. It always damages but you can do it, you start changing, two, three, four people... there's nothing left of the beginning, it's not the same.

Nick Sheppard: There would have never been a Clash without Joe. There couldn't be.

Some would say there was never a Clash without Mick and certainly history's been rewritten to that effect and I wouldn't disagree with them to be honest. I don't think that the band I was in was the real Clash, you know? It wasn't a bad band but The Clash were Mick, Joe, Paul and Topper and I don't have any problem with that but there would never - you couldn't have gone, formed a band and call it The Clash without Joe Strummer, you just couldn't do it.

AND ANOTHER THING...

Tymon Dogg: The Clash were actually a manufactured band, this is the paradox of it... Can't be that many manufactured bands that go on to get the recognition, not just the recognition but to be considered one of the bands with more integrity. So they did pretty well to survive.

Nick Sheppard: The Clash I played in was a fabrication, you know? It was me, it was this guy, and it was this drummer but the school of thought is that The Clash were always a fabrication, they were a band that was kind of made by - well if you listen to Bernie he invented the World but he certainly takes this credit for getting Joe and putting him with Mick.

Pete Howard: I think The Clash as a band were doomed by virtue of Bernie's interference and Topper's drug problem. I don't think there was ever gonna be a way that you would be able to reconcile those things but I think that was the band that was supposed to be.

Norman Watt-Roy: The Clash were four guys, man, that were important you know? And it worked, it was that magic that happens when those four guys got together, they just looked good - great! And it was just the right time. Once that had gone...

Rudy Fernandez: Joe and those guys and Mick, Paul and Topper they like you know, they raised a flag, you know? It was time for change. And they were the band.

Pat Gilbert: I think the musical aspect is key to the whole thing because at the end of the day they were a band, and I think once a bunch of guys can't get into the same room together and make the same sort of music that everyone likes you know, it's gonna fall apart very quickly which is exactly what happened.

Vince White: What happened when Mick Jones left? Not a lot, just happened. It was the same thing: running around on stage like fucking monkeys playing it and making a loud guitar sound!

Mick Jones: Much later on you sort of think: oh yeah I would have done it different or you might have done it different but I don't think the outcome would have been any different even if you had 'cause it's inevitable.

Pearl Harbor: It's just a natural progression, at the beginning they were brilliant and at the end they were grabbing at different straws to try to keep the band going 'cause Joe and Paul really wanted to, and it didn't really work, but they tried. But I don't see it as so much a mystery that you know, when a new band, new movement, Punk was new, that when you get a little bit older you can't be a fucking crazy ass Punk unless you are a loser.

Viv Albertine: You know it's funny how society takes something, absorbs it and sort of devalues it and takes all the sort of 'oomph' out of it and makes it banal and that kind of happened with Punk and it had to happen with Punk but I think you can see over the last thirty years the sort of real core of it has influenced a lot of people, a lot of young people, and in fact the sort of strength of it, it was so in your face Punk that it couldn't be accepted and diluted too much and it's taken almost thirty years to become acceptable and to become sort of woven back into music and some of the ideals to be taken on board.

Chris Salewicz: Because of the multiplicity of sources that they used, it spread out very, very much. Young kids love The Clash, kids love The Clash you know? Not just teenagers, even younger than teenagers, they love The Clash, it's somehow lasted. And it's lasted because of the great truths in that music and also the wit with which those lyrics and music is delivered and kind of makes you smile. And great truths, you know, told with a joke, tend to last.

Viv Albertine: Well I could be sort of flippant and say: well look the whole Clash arc was, you know, a bunch of scruffy boys, poor, playing guitars in their bedrooms, form a band, turn into a big Rock band, have their little squabbles and break up. You know, it's happened a million times before but on another hand I think they - you know there was great songwriting, there was a lot of passion, much deeper, better songs, much deeper passion than most bands ever - so that takes them and elevates them and makes them transcend that rather sort of corny little arc that I could have laid over them.

Ray Jordan: The Clash to me was the best Rock'n'Roll band, live band when they were hot. I don't think you can get a better atmosphere than that. And they knew how to satisfy their people. It's the only band I know who would try to get people in through the back door or anything, help out people, you know they don't just jump in their car and walk away. They even had people sleep in their rooms. I thought it was weird but that's what they wanted so...

Chris Townsend: they spoke for the working class and they spoke for human rights and they certainly took the responsibility of showing young people a direction. They supported a lot of things based around the humanistic attitude to life and they explored a lot of areas that bands hadn't gone to before.

Pearl Harbor: They were a gang... their ideal was kind of a bit like Robin Hood, you know they were people for the people, they weren't interested in being rich Rock'n'Roll assholes, well maybe towards the end some of that changed a little bit, God bless them, but at the beginning it all started out that they were you know, this gang of people who were interested in the politics of England and just being for the kids, everything was for the kids and for the people, it wasn't to make money in their pockets you know. Although they started out poor and they wanted money, it's when the money came in the picture that things changed but that's not that unusual...

Paul Simonon: I'm surprised it lasted as long as it did, from day one there was always - I mean, me and Mick used to have a lot of rows with each other, well for example in recording studios, it was endless, arguments about the sound of the bass or God knows what, arguments all along the route of The Clash, you know?

Chris Salewicz: I'm not surprised that The Clash are number three. I mean, it's The Beatles, The Rolling Stones and The Clash and that's widely acknowledged as that. I mean they were that great, they were that fantastic, extraordinary group as Bernie Rhodes would say, 'It is a very creative situation' and it was!

Mike Laye: I could never pin Bernie down to be either a revolutionary who was trying to use The Clash as a political tool... or whether he was a hustler who was using the tones and the feelings of the time to sell records. I could never decide that, whatever that ambivalence was, the way that he didn't deliver on either, because he certainly didn't deliver the social revolution that he continually talked about nor did he make the loads of money that you would think the marketing was all in aid of. That, to me, infected the band, that went into the band.

Tymon Dogg: They did what they did and I think people should be grateful for that!

Ray Jordan: Most of the people I know will tell you that that band changed their lives.

Mick Jones: Yes so we did something good, obviously, and we should leave it at that.

Chris Salewicz: As Kosmo Vinyl said to me, you know, 'Bernie was responsible for the greatest piece of art of 1977' and he also says, 'And largely through his own fault no one is aware of his influence on that'.

Chris Salewicz: When groups break up it's often very difficult for the various members, and they often take years to come down from it and sometimes they don't succeed at all. So Joe's certainly got that going, but also the terrible guilt for having kicked Mick out. You know, 'I was the one who blew it through classic hubris'... Plus his parents both died in quick succession and he's prone to depression anyway. And basically he really goes into one...

Chris Salewicz: ...But Joe really did, in his heart of hearts, still want to get The Clash back together.

AFTERWORD

John Turnbull: Tell him about when we pretended to bust The Clash at Wessex!

Mickey Gallagher: Oh yeah ... do you know that story? We were doing *I Want To Be Straight* with Ian Dury and we'd all got these police costumes. We were doing TV all dressed up as policemen - *I Want To Be Straight*, you know? And after - I had a session at the Wessex Studio afterwards, and they wanted Davy, the sax player, to go as well. So we all went, all piled in the car and we had this big blue Volvo, we put all the helmets on the back seat, went in the uniform, drove up in North London and when we got there we thought: wow, this is a good laugh. You know, we put the helmets on, run in and bust them.

Mick Jones: They kind of came running down the stairs and it looked like a police raid and we were all like: my God, we're being raided!

Mickey Gallagher: They freaked! They were just like: wow! You know, they really thought - 'cause if you see somebody with a policeman's uniform, you don't see the person, you just see the uniform. So there's all these policemen around everywhere, about five of us went up there and all of us were running around...

Norman Watt-Roy: 'You stay there! You, stay there!' And they stayed there!

Mickey Gallagher: I walked into Wessex and I saw Mick sort of wandering across the studio with a huge spliff in his hand and I went: 'YOU!' And there was fucking sparks going... And no one knew where Joe was 'cause he was sort of hiding in this bunker he'd made - and everybody got over it after you know, about fifteen minutes, everyone's 'ha ha ha' in the control room ... but nobody'd thought to tell Joe that it wasn't real so he was still sitting in the bunker with all his stash around him ...'what am I gonna do? The place is full of policemen!' Davy started playing and this cabbie, this cab driver, came in to pick someone up and he's standing there waiting and says, 'Sir, there's a policemen doing a saxophone solo'... And then Joe came in and he started beating Davy up! The cab driver just backed out, wow! He's off, he's away... oh some good fun, yeah we had some good fun...

DEDICATED TO

JOE STRUMMER, RAY LOWRY,

MIKEY DREAD, GUY STEVENS,

HENRY BOWLES AND NICK HAWKINS...

R.I.P.

About the Author

Danny Garcia was born in Barcelona. He started writing for the Spanish music press in 1990, interviewing The Cramps' Lux Interior and Poison Ivy. He has since contributed to numerous publications in several countries.

In the early 2000's Danny Garcia developed a series of documentaries for BTV (Barcelona's local TV station) depicting the local Hip Hop scene in chapters: b-boys, graffiti artists, MC's, DJ's and producers. Following this experience, Danny took on producing and directing his own films.

The Rise and Fall of The Clash was his first major production, a film that deals with the obscure end of the band that was one of Danny's favourites as a kid.

The search for the inside story took him on a strange, compelling adventure, that is related in the first part of the book.

Acknowledgements

Don Letts, Johnny Green, Bernard Rhodes, Sharon Rhodes, Mick Jones & The Rock & Roll Public Library, Nick Headon, Lucinda Mellor, Pockets, Trish Whelan @ Strummerville, Viv Albertine, Ray Jordan, Samuel Lowry, Terry Chimes, Tymon Dogg, Susan de Muth, Pearl Harbor, Jock Scot & Family, Dan Donovan, Chris Salewicz, Kris Needs, Mickey Gallagher, Norman Watt-Roy, Vince White, Nick Sheppard, Pete Howard, Vic Godard, Fayney, Barry "Scratchy" Myers, Rudy Fernandez, Mark Helfond, Jesús Arias, Mike Laye & Family, Chris Townsend @ MAP Studio Cafe, Kentish Town, Julian & Jackie @ See Gallery, Desmond Coy, César Méndez, Chris Knowles, Ana Bomboi & Paula de Langhe Bomboi, Varuni Siauw & Noni Siauw, Diego de Lippo, Professor Angel Sound, Andrew Matey, Joe Rebel, Ralph Heibutzki, Phil Mcillmurray, Juan José García, Vanessa d'Amelio, Justin Mozart, Travis Franks, Tracy Franks, Rebeca Gálvez, Joan Garcia Grau, Sergi Garcia, Paul Caren, Anthony Pepitone, Joe Streno, Pat Gilbert, Robin Banks, Eddie King, Tim @ theclashblog.com, Maria Gallagher, Iñigo Espada @ Espacio Compartido and everybody I've met along the way who helped me put this together. Thank you!